-The Hate You Breed-

Overcoming Ignorance

Written

By

Raul Cantu

<u>Table of Contents:</u>

<u>Dedication</u>

This book is dedicated to a divided humanity. It is a guide to bring us to understanding our inner connection to one another so that we can live in harmony. Finally, we are awaking now to the universal truths that are hidden within each of us. This will be known as the Awakening Era. Together we will unlock the key to creating Heaven on Earth. Our goal should be to do everything we can so that we can to leave earth better than what we found it.

To my loving family, my wife Tearsa and our three wonderful sons; Damien, Rowen and Zayden, and my daughter-in law Jasmine; you all are my true inspiration for wanting to make this world a safer and more creative place. I have been blessed to be a part of your lives in this lifetime and I wish you all, a long, happy, life filled with love, peace, and prosperity. Through these pages my hope is that we, the human race will no longer tolerate weapons of mass destruction, nor advance the effects of global warming, and stop the hate; so that future generations can live without the fear of death, because humanity deserves better than that!

INTRODUCTION

On September 11, 2001, Americans were caught unexpectedly by a new form of energy that knows no boundaries. Suddenly "the enemy" was no country or a certain race or culture; but instead, a sporadic attacker that loves their God more than life. They entered America, not to live the American dream, but to destroy it.

These cowards infiltrated America from within, trained in our facilities, until they revealed unto our eyes the most gruesome attack in our countries modern-day history. Blinded by the imaginary boundaries of their mind, these cowards transited our loved ones into missiles of terror. They did this to us America because they felt that our government had done them wrong. They said the cause of that terror was due to our government meddling in foreign affairs, trying to gain power through unauthentic means.

Today the biggest threat that lies ahead of us is the total self-destruction of all things due to our mass destructive weapons. We the people have paid for them and in doing so, we face the possibility of destroying this wondrous planet. All of which is caused by fear, ego and racism.

Humanity has forgotten the most significant language of all; the universal language within - our common sense. If we do nothing but sit around awaiting the end of time, then we have failed to grasp the true purpose of life. As they pronounce endlessly that these are the end of times and that it is a good thing, because the end brings back Christ, I ask you, my fellow humans to open your eyes, before they are shut forever!

I will ask you to listen to your heart and intuition and enter the realm of reality. What you are about to read is the most compelling information that has ever been composed in our history. I ask you to be open minded and trust your soul to these universal truths that are about to be revealed to you.

I wrote the essence of this literature when I was young, it came to me in a vision. I knew in my heart that the information contained in these pages would transform the way we think, the way we live and alter the course of this journey we call life. Ultimately, I knew that the knowledge that I am about to share with you was so <u>significant</u> that those who came before me were murdered for trying to disclose this information.

I wrote this book, published it and then pulled it from production, only to store it in a closet for over 30 years. Now it is time to unleash this knowledge, to a struggling and divided world. Since the inception of Humanity, many great minds have come forth with what I call universal truths and auspicious visions of freedom.

In America alone, Abraham Lincoln, Martin Luther King Jr., John F Kennedy, and even the great musician John Lennon who dared to dream of all of us living as one; were just a few of the chosen ones that were killed by narrow-minded men who did not want to see freedom flourish. They did not want this positive state of mind known as freedom to spread to the masses, so they destroyed the messenger, but the message lives on, because it is written within each of us.

In 1776, a political philosopher and writer by the name of Thomas Paine graced us with a pamphlet titled "<u>COMMON SENSE</u>". Because of this literature, we were able to remember the reason humans traveled to America to begin with – for Freedom. We wanted a better life and so our founding fathers were inspired by the words of Thomas Paine and what emerged was the Declaration of Independence. Since then, we have forgotten the intentions of our founding fathers, but more importantly, we have forgotten the intentions of freedom and liberty that are inscribed in our souls. We were born to be free. We've just forgotten how to use our mind and think for ourselves.

Global human consciousness does not die when our bodies pass away, it is collected and available for each new generation. We know collectively that slavery is wrong, but we also know that just because we have come to our senses and abolished it, that racism no longer exist; because it does exist and thrives in America and all over the world. It's there, it just shifts from this group of people to another set of people.

Ultimately, we are trying to reach the greatest intention of the universe, and that is to be totally free so that we can expand our love and consciousness. That is the ultimate vision that I call the Auspicious Vision. It's a vision of freedom for all; but we cannot get there yet because we are full of ego, pride and sadly, blinded by imaginary boundaries.

In this book, you will discover that the divinity is not out there in some unknown place, but rather, it is within you. We have the power to save or destroy this beautiful planet. In these pages lies the keys to peace, happiness, and prosperity on a personal and world-wide level. Here is the formula for Heaven on Earth. Join me now, on the greatest journey that one can take in their lifetime; a journey that will ultimately set us free!

Better to die fighting for freedom
then be a prisoner all the days of
your Life!

-Bob Marley

-**Doomsday**-

Throughout the history of mankind prophets, astrologers and bible believers have predicted when and how our world shall end. Some of the most famous calculations of doomsday often indicate a great abundant force entering the earth's atmosphere – unconfined. Take for instance, in the year '1939' Americans listened terrified as "<u>WAR OF THE WORLDS</u>" broadcasted live via the radio.

This story was nothing more, nor less than one man's creative imagination, who cunningly combined both fantasy and reality and presented it as the truth. He was able to do this, by tapping into America's fear of the unknown. Since then, there have been countless movies and documentaries revealing a common fear of aliens attempting to erase humanity and conquer earth.

Other famous doomsday predictions include bringing forth "the end" by an immense asteroid collision. Scientist are convinced that this is what occurred 65 million years ago, and it eradicated the great dinosaur era. Many believe this will inevitably be the demise of humanity as well.

Through the revelations of his imagination, emerged Michael Nostradamus perhaps the most famous prophet to ever live. He is believed to have foretold such events as; The French Revolution, The Rise and Fall of both Napoleon and Hitler and to some the horrid terror from the sky know to us now as the events that took place on 9/11. You decide for yourself -July 1999, In quatrain 10-72, Nostradamus Visions:

L'an mil neuf cens nonante neuf sep mois
Du ciel viendra grand Roy Deffraieur
Resusciter le grand Roy d'Angolmois.
Auant apres Mars regner par bon heur.

The year 1999, seven months'
From the sky will come a great king of terror:
To bring back to life the great king of the Mongols,
before and after Mars to reign by good luck.

- Nostradamus

For many, this is the man who saw tomorrow; yet what occurred on September 11, 2001, was not the end, as predicted by him or anyone else. This day will forever go down as one of the saddest days in our country's history, yet it did not end us. What emerged through such a horrific act was only the beginning of an inner connection to one another; as we entered unknowingly into the era known as – *the Awakening!*

As you can see, we have managed to escape the total destruction of earth foretold by numerous prophecies; the question is why do we suggest earth will end from an outer source, rather than suggesting what we can do to prevent an end? Are we that blind? Most humans fail to realize the true crisis earth is facing right now. As you read this sentence, billions of people feel hopeless towards the fate of our future or do not care, yet it is in our hands.

Most people are blinded by fantasy and programmed to deny reality. Planet Earth will not end because of a falling star or an asteroid; nor will end by invading aliens. We as humans are amongst the most intelligent, yet ignorant species to ever exist on this planet. If and when, this world shall end, it will be due to the <u>thoughts</u> of man! Please re-read this sentence because it is one of the most significant sentences in this book. No other form of life can destroy what humans are destroying – the Earth.

Our war technology is beyond the boundaries of our control, and we have taken this immature warfare to an extent of total self-destruction. It is the first step in committing suicide as a whole; the next step may be our last. To be or not to be, is still an unanswered question!

We have reached a point in life where a decision must be made. We can sit around awaiting the end of the time because we have somehow tied it to the return of Jesus, or we can save and recreate life as never before seen. We can create heaven on earth, so that each generation to come can inherit a better world than the last or you can put this book down right now and continue to do nothing.

I believe the world and humanity will conclude soon if we do not spread this vital message! You are reading this literature for a reason and in that reason lies the power to save the world. As miniscule as it may seem; the key or secret to saving our world lies in the power to educate ourselves. By educating ourselves we release the fear of not knowing. Without fear, humans will be at peace with themselves, as well as with others. It is of great importance that you remember this and pass it on to others.

-<u>Imaginary Boundaries</u>-

We are living in a world of ignorance. This ignorance is passed down through the imaginary boundaries we are born into or later recruited into. We must open our eyes and learn to see past these imaginary boundaries if we are to survive. Imaginary boundaries have been the cause of all violence and war. Humans do not recognize this, for they are blinded by it. What are imaginary boundaries? They are thoughts, beliefs, traditions, and customs. They deprive one of proper self-education and more disturbingly they are the cause of oppressing human rights.

Imaginary boundaries are intangible forces of negative energy capable of causing humans to be blind to the realities of life and laws and love of nature. The imaginary boundaries that I warn you of are especially associated and are deeply rooted within cultural, ethnic, political, and religious societies. There are many others, however the four mentioned here are the most influential and powerful of all imaginary boundaries to ever be created by the human mind and passed down through the ages as creeds, customs, beliefs, opinions, and laws.

In this book you will learn to view life as it should be seen. Far too often, humans get caught up in the web of imagination; the only way to escape this mind-made web is to view all things true and from within.

When we are born, we are tethered together by our common sense; however, as we age, we tend to disengage from it because of the imaginary boundaries in our mind. We separate ourselves from others. Very few can view the world without being blinded or influenced by these harsh imaginary boundaries. Most people remain caught up in society and thus blinded by reality.

We the people must *discontinue* to dispute whether we are Democratic or Republican, Jewish or Christian, American or Russian, heterosexual or homosexual, transgender or cisgender, or any other imaginary boundaries humans tend to argue over. Imaginary boundaries are taught beliefs and opinions; they are silly labels we give each other. They are created by the finite mind to gain control over others and build one up through unauthentic means. What they do is allow humans to cast judgement on others and categorize humans and create a hierarchy in society.

In short, many creations and laws of nature have emerged through people influenced by imaginary boundaries that provide the mind meaning and answers to some of life's most challenging questions. Many have been able to bring forth universal truths and universal laws and we are grateful for this knowledge; however, most of it is mixed with fantasy.

In most cases, the meanings of truth differ throughout each imaginary bound derived society. Thus, when we are born, we are labeled and judged by what we will be <u>taught</u> to believe in, the color of our skin, and by the land and culture in which we are unknowingly born into.

Yet behind all the names and labels that have been created to separate us lies this reality; namely, that we are all one kind - the humankind. We are human beings with a mind, body, and soul. This is all we truly own; however, humans tend to claim exceedingly more, especially those that grant themselves power over nature.

People blinded by societies who struggle for power and reassurance in their beliefs are those most blinded by the realities and truths of life. Only those who can see beyond the imaginary boundaries that humans have cursed themselves with, can comprehend the reality of this philosophy.

Many great people have come forward before me and before their time with universal truths and clear visions of freedom for all. Such humans have inspired me with their ability to un-blind the masses from control, dictatorship, and the imaginary boundaries in which derail us from living our optimal life!

"Our suffering is caused by the mind –
by a mind that insist on having preferences
and will not allow others to be just as they are".

Dr. Wayne W Dyer
"EVERYDAY WISDOM"

-<u>Making Sense</u>-

We are a species made up of over six and a half billion individuals. We are intended to be born with seven key senses, yet most of us only use five; they are sight, touch, smell, hear, and taste. The sixth and seventh senses are often dismissed due to the means in which we receive them. The sixth sense was eloquently brought into light by an American author named Napoleon Hill in his brilliant masterpiece "<u>THINK AND GROW RICH</u>". Mr. Hill described the sixth sense as the portion of the sub-conscious mind referred to as *Creative Imagination*. He also described it as the receiving set through which ideas, plans and thoughts flash into the mind sometimes referred to as hunches or intuition.

The sixth sense is responsible for the evolution of cave people progressing into modern day civilizations. Your favorite poems, songs, prayers, art, books, and movies were all created through the power of creative imagination. All things creative are possible only through the faculty of the mind known as the sixth sense.

Everything <u>ever</u> created by humans came to them first in the form of a thought, vision, or idea. Humans can bring into reality anything that their brains can conceive and believe. Any person can tap into the wealth that is infinite intelligence through his or her creative imagination, where all things are possible.

Pause for just a minute and look at your surroundings, distinguish what nature provides and what humans have created through nature. Our world is filled with creative ideas that have been transited and manifested into their physical equivalency.

Humans are capable of bringing and/or transforming the intangible into reality through the sixth sense. The clothes on your body and this book both started off as a thought through creative imagination. The sixth sense is the most significant wonder in this world, for without it, the human species would simply wander. Moreover, we are the only species to ever exist that can shape the face of the earth with just our thoughts!

In opposite of creative imagination is negative thinking. These thoughts are brought on by negative emotions, such as fear, hate, envy, anger, and greed. Through the power of the sub-conscience mind, we can grasp and transits into reality both negative or positive thoughts and ideas. Unfortunately, the sub-conscious mind does not detect what is right or wrong. It merely works as a tool or platform to transmit the intangible to its material form. Hence, many thoughts and ideas have altered the appearance and living standards for the better, yet not all ideas have proved to be beneficial to the safety and wellbeing of humanity and earth.

This leads me to the seventh sense. It is a sense once whispered by Thomas Paine in 1776 to an emerging America and seemingly unheard of since then. It is the sense that can save earth from the terrifying revelations of doomsday and continued acts of terrorism on our country.

On September 11, 2001, it became apparent that the seventh sense had awoken within each of us, for on that unforgettable day, most of humanity was connected through the universal language within. The seventh sense is naturally instilled in each of us; however, it is not simple to accept it and/or to connect to it because of our imaginary boundaries and other distractions like drugs and alcohol.

Once we do connect to it and begin to use it, it renders humans with an inner judgement of truth and reality and what is safe and what is dangerous. If used properly; you become truly aware of what is right and what is wrong. It will help you determine what is positive and negative, and what is certain and not for certain. One thing that is for certain is that it is NOT used when carrying out negative ideas into their physical equivalency. Such as, in the case of war and performing acts of terrorism and murder.

Sometimes we are demanded or advised to do certain things which we know deep within should not be allowable. If we choose to follow through and do them anyway; we choose to ignore the seventh sense. The seventh sense is our common sense -yet, in this day in age, it should be called uncommon sense for it is rarely used by humans as it should be. Those who choose not to use and/or harness the power of our common sense are often those most blinded by man-made laws, man-made drugs and/or the imaginary boundaries in our minds. Which are often those who easily fall prey to conspiracy theories, brainwashing, and big lies.

Imaginary boundaries have the power to conquer your mind and cripple your judgement. They have the power to rob common sense from within you and replace it with laws, rules, and commandments of opinion. Opinions are made by the finite mind. Humans have yet to discover that the laws of nature differ than the laws of man. Such individuals are untrue to themselves in believing they can betray nature.

Just as the earth continuously spins, so do our contributions. For those of you who break the laws of nature, common sense should tell you "What goes around comes around" and when it does it usually comes with a vengeance. What we do to nature will be done onto us, for we are one! If we destroy and betray nature, we destroy and betray ourselves.

We are an undeniable living product of nature and nature thrives within each of us. We are connected to nature and every other living organism on this planet. Therefore, deep within you lies all the answers to what is right and wrong, true, and untrue.

This is called your common sense and in a time such as ours, where people are so blinded by imaginary boundaries and try desperately to plant their seeds of doubt and false predictions, conspiracies, and fear; it becomes extremely difficult to properly use your very own true judgement within – your common sense, but that's about to change!

"You have to leave
the city of your comfort
and go into the wilderness,
of your intuition.

What you'll discover –
will be wonderful.
What you'll discover, will be yourself."

Alan Aloa

-<u>Educational Fallacy</u>-

Common sense in most schools is avoided due to the influence of imaginary boundaries. I say nothing bad about the elementary levels in school, for we must learn our basics; how to read, write, and experience communication skills and above all, the exercising of creative imagination. The fallacy begins towards the later years of school, when students are prepared to need college rather than preparing them for the real world and how to succeed in doing what they love.

Please make no mistake that I am grateful for the production of specialized knowledge, for we need our doctors, lawyers, teachers and all the other curriculum which leads humans to the wonderful professions of this world. I also know that a degree or certificate does not always validate a person's success, intelligence, and overall happiness. Each year students are guided to some type of specialized knowledge or training.

Charter schools have exploded in every big city and their narrative is to prepare students for college. These schools are taking so many students from public schools, making the charter schools the exact same as the public schools. Unfortunately, many of them will realize when it is too late that this path is not always the right path for everyone.

It has been estimated that college will be one of the largest expenses a human will encounter in their lifetime. When one chooses to attend college or a university, he or she is paying to be taught. Millions of Americans pay for a good education, but a good education comes from within, it's wanting to learn about the things we are most interested and passionate about, the subjects we desire most and the things we love.

I encourage you to view paying for an education as a choice. If it is really what you want to do, to get to where you need to get, then by all means, do it. But it is not the *only* path to success! You must learn to seek any subjects or information that truly interests you. You cannot be influenced by other minds. No one knows you better than yourself and no one can make life worth living but yourself!

Understand now that every person you come into contact with is seeking the opportunity to accumulate money and success; many succeed, unfortunately most do not. When the idea arose to charge for an education, it was brought to the mind in an attempt to earn riches and every course one takes builds wealth for that one idea. Great ideas can long outlive the finite minds that they come from.

Henry Ford made the decision to stop going to school while he was in elementary school, nor did he attend college. In today's world we would call this absurd, and his parents would be put in jail for allowing this to occur. Vicente Fernandez, perhaps the most famous Mariachi of all time, did the same, stopped going to elementary school because he knew his passion was singing. Yet both of these men became extremely successful in their calling. This is because, written within our souls is a code that we cannot deny, if we do, we have failed to listen within. Our common sense and creative imagination can guide us only as far as the imaginary boundaries in our mind limit us.

Have the courage
to follow your
heart and intuition.
They somehow
know what you
truly want to become.

-Steve Jobs

-<u>Listen Within</u>-

Everyone has a calling in his or her life and until each individual finds his or her true calling, his or her soul will remain unsatisfied and unhappy. This is true even if one attains the highest degree in life; if they are *not* doing what they love they will remain unsatisfied in life. If you can see beyond imaginary boundaries, you will see a place that humans have created, and which contains more information and knowledge than any college course can offer. To enter into this marvelous palace is simple, you need no previous training, no money, and all are welcome.

The more you enter this door; you will begin to realize that anything and everything can be learned here. As Napoleon Hill states, experience has that the best educated people are often those who are known as "self-made" or self-educated.

If knowledge is power, then the most powerful place on earth is a place where all races and ages are welcome. It is a place that is often underrated and overlooked, yet it contains more specialized knowledge and creative imagination in one building than any one person can imagine. This place is the physical version of our sixth sense. This place can spark ingenuity and inspiration in each of us and help point us directly to our calling, that is if we can learn to see the value and treasures of our public libraries. Can you attain a degree in the library? No, but you can learn who you truly are and what your purpose is.

Here, the greatest minds of today and throughout history have left behind treasures of knowledge in every genre and in every entity in life, so that we do not need to fear the unknown. You may be asking what this has to do with saving this planet. It has everything to do with it, because when a mind is educated, humans no longer live in fear.

The word intolerance means that one's narrow mindedness has stopped them from acquiring continued knowledge. It is the thought that many get once they have reached the pinnacle of specialized knowledge and or training in any one field. It is the idea that one has already learned all he or she needs to learn in their lifetime. For instance, a psychologist may feel that they cannot learn more, since they have already mastered the mind, or when someone believes that the only knowledge they need is in the bible; these are a few examples of intolerance.

(11)

The most damaging forms of intolerance are those people blinded by religious, professional, and political differences of opinion. The brain must never take a break from learning, or it will produce negativity out of pure *neglect*. It is essential for our future that human beings learn to continuously educate themselves; do not deny yourself this universal truth! Just as the human body must consume in order to survive, it must also release that which has entered. If the body is not fed or becomes weak and dehydrated, negative reactions will inevitably occur.

No species on earth is exempt to the laws of nature and it's cycles. The brains of humans are unlike the brains of any other species. No species consumes as much energy as we do, thus our brains are of no exception to the laws of nature. If you fail to continuously feed the brain knowledge, then the brain will become weak and most susceptible to negative emotions, thoughts, and suggestions

To truly understand this law of nature is to discover the root cause of most violence and ignorance. Evidence to support this law is that 80% of the individuals in prison are illiterate, meaning they are uneducated. To be self-educated is to enjoy and comprehend the information of your choice. The library can be a powerhouse to stay constantly connected but remember that imaginary boundaries can derail us at any time. We must learn to see what the actual truth is, and what are big lies and misinformation. We need to distinguish what are the laws of nature and the laws of man. If we can learn to see beyond our imaginary boundaries, we will see the greatest truth of all time; namely, that we are all one connected in harmony with the universe.

There is no longer the need to engage in these power struggles and kill each other over our stale beliefs and meaningless labels. To be one is to be free from all imaginary boundaries and free from war. I know that it is difficult to detach the strings in which imaginary boundaries hold us by; although if we do not, earth will inevitably end, and all this will be caused by our fear of not acknowledging and using our common sense.

> "A musician must make music,
> An artist must paint,
> A poet must write,
> If is to be ultimately at peace with himself"
>
> Abraham Maslow

(12)

Plato once said; "To find yourself is the greatest accomplishment of all." He was right, but in order to find ourselves, we must search. If you fail to search, you fail to find it. Children will be fed to a certain age then they must learn to feed themselves. We must learn to become our own teachers and continuously self-educate ourselves. Only then will we be free from the wraths of the unknown and the intolerance we've grown to know.

The Dalai Lama, when asked what
surprised him most about humanity,
answered "Man! Because he sacrifices
his health in order to make money.
Then he sacrifices money to recuperate his health.
And then he is so anxious about
the future that he does not enjoy the present;
the result being that he does not live
in the present or the future; he lives as if
he is never going to die, and then dies having
never really lived."

- Dali Lama

-Unauthentic Power-

The struggles within humanity seem to be never ending, even in modern times man has not learned from his past. After reading the first chapter of this literature, you learned that it is an option to pay for an education. Even if one receives the highest degree of education, he or she is not exempt from teaching themselves continuously. With that said, emerged a society blinded by imaginary boundaries. This society is the most harmful society to ever emerge.

I cannot help but feel empathetic towards young adults that are recruited by this society in this country for war. My grandfather, my father and most of my uncles were all recruited into this society. I have nothing against those who serve, and I am grateful for their service. My concern is about the leaders of this country who get us caught up in the wrong services like unnecessary wars. These so-called leaders have used funds to produce the technology needed to end this race!

Americans pay the Internal Revenue Service trillions of dollars each year and each year we drive ourselves one step closer to destroying our future. It is a situation that most are forced into. Many of which complain constantly over the amount of money being used on welfare. These individuals are most blinded to see the true concerns we are faced with, such as the hundreds of billions of dollars used to manufacture warfare. American Taxpayers pay the entire payroll for the millions of individuals who are trained to defend our country. We feed, shelter, clothe, provide medical and dental care, and pay half the bill for childcare. The money granted to those soldiers who choose to attend college through the military, comes from Americans who are forced to pay.

This path is actually a top option for both the parent and the student when discussing a successful future and for many it is, especially for those who do not have to see a day of war. However, we have fallen into a hierarchy system, where the government controls its own people. Yet the entire government and it's dependents live off of the money, taxpayers are forced to pay each year. Thus, they work for you. Sadly, somewhere along the line, between 1776 and now, we have managed to let our government control us. This power thirsty society is one of the wealthiest and most powerful of all imaginary bound societies to ever exist.

"We the people" pay the political society trillions of dollars, then these blinded leaders that we elect, distribute those funds as they wish. Much of which is passed onto our military officials. These blinded humans have in their possession all the money needed to produce any and all negative ideas into their physical equivalency. Man's eagerness to progress in the field of war has led to the invention of some of the cruelest technology on earth.

Understand this, all weapons are created and intended to <u>KILL</u> life easily and effortlessly, and that they do! They are not made to improve the quality of life, to heal or to increase peace and safety. Their sole purpose is to mass-murder and destroy as much as possible with no consciousness or little remorse.

Through the years we have paid for guns, battleships, submarines, aircrafts, land tanks, bombs, missiles, weapons of mass destruction and any new technology brewing in secret as you read this literature. All of these weapons came to the mind through man's ego and negative emotions; mainly out of fear, hate, anger, and revenge.

These weapons have been produced by progressive countries for a purpose and if we do not speak up now, that purpose will destroy *all* us completely. It is time to visualize the reality that humans have bought themselves into, in the making of nuclear weapons, we, (the United States <u>alone</u>) are now capable of destroying this beautiful and irreplaceable planet more than 10 times over.

Please understand that this is not a joke, or my opinion, but sadly, our gruesome reality. If the world ends, as we know it, it will not come from out there, but rather from within. Therefore, these kings of Terror that we have created make this society the most dangerous and blinding of all time.

By creating weapons of mass-destruction; Countries like America, Russia and China have won the war of wars, as well as the war of ignorance. In fact, the only thing left to conquer is man's own <u>stupidity</u>! This competition of man versus man has reached a conclusion with only two options. The first comes from an Old Chinese proverb:

> "Unless we change the direction we are headed,
> we might end up where we are going."

It is no secret that our so-called leaders of today are leading us to the end, by means of global war and/or global warming. Throughout history we have given all imaginary bound derived societies the opportunity to create life based on views and opinions of their society's belief. All have failed and brought forward this egotistical dilemma we are now faced with.

Through their blindness and arrogance, we are now locked in an endless struggle for power - *Unauthentic Power.* Why do we allow mass destructive weapons to even exist on earth? Fear; most taxpayers fear the government and they are aware of it and as long as they detect the fear in you, they will continue to do as they please with our countless amounts of money. Failure to pay your taxes results in the loss of your home and property; paying your taxes results in the possible loss of our world. Which is of more importance to you, where are headed?

Which leads us to reveal the second option; a method that has been ignored for centuries. Sadly, due to illiteracy and the imaginary boundaries that construe our logical thinking; many Americans are clueless when it comes to our country's history. In the Declaration of Independence, Thomas Jefferson knew that the government would eventually bite the hand that feeds it. Thus, he wrote "Whenever a government becomes destructive of these ends, (Life, Liberty, and the pursuit of happiness) it is the right of the people to alter or abolish it, and to institute new government. Laying down its powers in such, as to them shall seem most likely to affect their safety and happiness."

If you comprehend this essential portion of the Declaration of Independence, then you obviously understand that life, liberty, and the pursuit of happiness comes before all! Does it bring you happiness to fund strangers from our government with an unlimited amount of wealth, only to create and house the deadliest technology to ever exist? By funding these weapons of mass destruction and other warfare technology, have we truly ensured life, liberty, and happiness for all?

Realize now that it is our responsibility to save our lives but also to ensure that we leave this world secure and safe for future generations to come. We must come together now more than ever, through our common sense. We must learn to accept as a reality that our government exists today, only because of taxpayer money.

The land you call home and the houses owned by any government affiliates belong to you. Mass destructive weapons belong to you too, you paid for them and now you must decide what will become of them. Understand that it is your money that can make or break any government. Therefore, you have the *power* to tell your employees what you would like done. As powerful as our government may seem, realize that they are individuals no different than you or me, with the exception that they are dependent upon you and me. This society needs you, not just for you money, but more than ever for your guidance. To speak out on behalf of nature is the only way for earth to continue on its natural course.

The Government has obviously abused what nature has given man and man has allowed himself to act upon his most negative thoughts and obsessions. They have combined just the correct elements needed to convert earth into a toxic existence. In an age such as ours; the most <u>significant</u> threat to ever exist on earth, goes greatly unacknowledged, as if no one truly cares, not just in our country, but around the world. We have become complacent into believing that there is no real treat of global war and global warming.

Much of the far right are so busy harassing immigrants, gays, transsexuals, and women's rights; yet, they do or say nothing to protect us from the real dangers that are impending on this world. Although you did not produce weapons of mass destructive, per se, you also took no part in protesting such negative inventions. For the purpose of saving humanity and the only *known* planet to offer life within our reach, humans from all languages must reach deep within their soul and learn to hear the most <u>important</u> language of all, the universal language within. Only then can we start the healing.

As we proceed forward, towards the future, we must not forget to pause and review the nature of our inventions and distinguish what stands in our way of life, liberty, and the pursuit of happiness. This must be done on a global level. Every human being is connected despite what race, religion, or culture we come from. If we can one day grasp this simplest of truths, then we as a species can conquer all of our pride and prejudice and learn to let go. We will no longer have to be trapped in vicious cycle where we are constantly trying to get our energy from each other by draining or overpowering one another and we will learn how to acquire *authentic power* from the genuine source that created us.

(17)

Knowing that we are all connected through our common sense with not just every human being on earth, but with all living things in this universe, including the universe itself, will release the fear of war, violence and ignorance and this will unlock the auspicious visions that we carry within.

Do not allow ignorant individuals (many of our world's leaders) to produce and maintain mass-destructive weapons for "just in case" reasons. Man has killed enough and if we do not erase these negatives from our reality and start educating ourselves, man will kill all! All of these precious moments will be lost in time. This is the biggest reality check that you will have to face in your life and the biggest hill that we must climb as a human race. We must stop viewing the world as dark place or that we are merely passing through; because this is our home and we only get one, so WAKE UP!

"Those who think that
The world is a dark place
are blind to the light
that might illuminate their lives"

Dr. Wayne W Dyer
"Everyday Wisdom"

(18)

-__Global Karma__-

Man has already demolished hundreds of millions of acres of existence, destroying most of the Earth's natural rain forest. According to Global Citizen, "roughly 64% of the world's tropical rainforest has been destroyed or degraded since pre-industrial times, that means that just 36% of the global rainforest remain." This ignorance is apparent because America has cut down most of the mature forest in which greeted European settlers in the seventeenth century.

Half of all the trees cut down by man are used to make paper. America's demand for wood products outweighs metals, plastics and cement combined. To meet our over-whelming demand, we allow and/or pay companies to go into forest that sustain life for more than half of all the plant and animal kingdoms. The effect is that every *single* day hundreds of plant and animal species go extinct, leading us to extinct 50,000 species each year.

The curse is a blinded humanity – the cure, is educating humanity! This is no opinion, but rather another harsh reality of the damage we are implicating to our earth. We often wonder if there will be cures for our more advanced forms of cancer, Aids and other terminal illnesses and the answer may lie in our inability to stop gutting away the insides of mother nature.

As terminal illnesses eat away within, so do we, to nature. We have become a form of cancer to Mother Nature. We have also limited our chances of finding certain cures with every species of plant we allow to become extinct and moreover, we may be generating new forms of illness's we cannot cure, control or comprehend.

"Massive deforestation is violating nature's natural virus protection mechanisms, putting the whole world at risk from potential new pathogens spreading from animals to humans," Krogh said from Global Citizen. "The aftermath of Covid-19 should bring rainforest protection to the top of the agenda of all policymakers and world leaders concerned about preventing the outbreak of new pandemics." Another words, new life forms are being created as we keep destroying and causing extinction in the forest. These life forms may not be good for us.

Still, we search for the cure and never question the cause. To find the cure and prevent terminal illness's from humanity; we must acknowledge and abide by the laws of nature and learn to listen within. All diseases and viruses are forms of <u>energy</u>. They are also messages from the universe. What we do to nature is being done to us. We are the creators of these diseases, no one else is doing this to us, but ourselves.

When we choose to pollute the air, while destroying the earth's forest, we are taking nature's air filters, her lungs. Without these massive trees both the land below and ozone above begin to deteriorate. As of today, this causes weather patterns to alter to places where they are not accustomed to it, like different regions that are now experiencing massive tornados or hurricanes that surge beyond; however, in the very near future, it will inevitably get worse – from "El Nino to El Diablo."

Blinded by their imaginary boundaries, humans have dumped tons of raw sewage and other hazardous materials into our once pristine oceans, lakes, and rivers; never comprehending the true consequences. The water in various parts of the world is contaminated so badly that people can no longer eat or drink from these waters for lifetimes to come. Each year it is estimated that we dump over 700 million gallons of oil into our oceans. We are creating a sludge of toxins.

There are portions of earth where man has prohibited himself to enter for thousands of years, when he decided to release radioactive particles, in the testing and meltdown of Nuclear Energy. Research the story of Chernobyl, and you will see a glimpse of the damage we are on path to inherit if we partake in nuclear war. It is said that this location; the area around Chernobyl will NOT be habitable again until 20,000 years from now. Is this the kind of earth that we want to leave behind to our children and grandchildren?

The human species has assaulted the forest, contaminated the waters and now we are eroding the ozone layer at an irreversible rate. Thus far, we have managed to pollute the land, the water and air; nature's mind, body, and soul. Why? Understand this, terminal illnesses, and new viruses like Covid 19 are new life forms emerging within us to destroy us; doing to us what we are doing to nature. If we protect and appreciate nature, then nature will provide protection for us.

(20)

We need to wake up and listen within, because most people do not care about the damages, we are causing. In fact, most people are encouraging more damages because it brings back Jesus.

Humans blinded by imaginary boundaries have granted power over all of nature and her creations. On our human journey through life, we have forgotten that we *need* nature, because we are a part of nature.

In all of the vast animal kingdom, only humans have the power to alter the face of earth. No other species can destroy the planet as we are doing, yet no other species can create such amazement upon her as we can. Just as we must embrace one another despite all the labels, we must learn to respect and embrace the spectacular forest, plants, and animals of this world. They were manifested into existence for a reason and humans have no right to extinct them, we just think we do. It is our hate and ignorance that is blinding us into our own demise, only our love and compassion can save us from the monsters that we have become.

Only after the last tree has
been cut down. Only after
the last river has been poisoned.
Only after the last fish has been
caught. Only then you will find
that money cannot be eaten.

- Cree Indian Prophecy

(21)

-<u>The Animal Kingdom</u>-

Since man's existence on earth, he has given himself permission to capture, test, crossbreed, clone, torture, murder and or keep in captivity the entire animal kingdom. At one point in life, when the Native Indians inhabited America, it was said that over 30 million bison roamed the great plains. The Natives used the skin of buffalo to provide shelter, by building tepees and used it to create clothing to keep warm. They did this but still kept their respect for bison and nature.

Then came along the settlers, who invaded North America with their guns and their mindset, killing almost all the bison, but a few hundred. These people killed the bison, not for clothes and resources but rather to let the Native Indian know they were in charge, and this could and would ultimately be their fate as well.

Countless animals are pouched each year alongside America's roads, as if hunters are starving to death. Man has taken this ignorance and proudly displays his killings upon his walls, as game trophies. Even the king of the jungle has been replaced by man as ruler of the land. In this age, humans neatly package and display edible animal parts into grocery stores for our convenience. It is how we have evolved and adapted as species in modern day societies.

Then there are those who cannot cook and there is nothing wrong with that, however they manage to survive by paying someone to do their cooking for them; by either take out, drive through or personal chef. Let's face it, we have made it easy, enabling modern day civilizations to pay rather than have to kill their food. This is human evolution and we have come a long way from our ancient human relatives.

Centuries ago, there were no options, today there should be no reason to kill, especially if you live in America, for the exception of those who still live off the land, or off grid, like our Natives once did. For decades, humans have often wondered, why is there so much violence within humanity? Leaders on the right struggle to find the answer to our mass shooting problem; they are quick to blame everyone else. Its "mental health, its video games, its race, it's because there are not enough good guys with guns".

In this literature, you will find true answers; unfortunately, many of you will not accept it at first. Why? Because we are blinded and programed to deny reality, especially those who are blinded by political and religious beliefs (imaginary boundaries).

The truth is so simple, yet so hard for us to grasp. Why does America have a massive problem with gun violence? Because there is easy _Access_ to guns; meaning, there are means of killing and murdering prey everywhere.

When Moses wrote Genesis, he gave humans dominion over the fish of the sea, the birds of the air and all animals that crawl on earth. Therefore, all those who believe that this is the actual word of God are given authority over nature, not by nature, but by man. Thus, for thousands of years, all that we have been taught to think has manifested into our reality. However, we have evolved into a more spiritual and modern human species, or at least we are trying to.

There is no longer the need to allow anybody the privilege of carrying guns in our cities. We are no longer in the barbaric days or stuck in the wild west days. We are here in the awakening process now, triumphing over corrupt politics and bad choices. No one has the right to kill nature when foods from all parts of the world can be shipped to us in sophistication.

Understand that weapons are created specifically to kill instantly, swiftly, and unconsciously. We have made killing each other, as easy as it is to photograph one another. We have made purchasing firearms as easy as it is to purchase groceries. It is time to rise up against gun manufacturers from producing and marketing these horrible inventions. As long as guns and bullets are being produced for any circumstances whatsoever, our streets, our schools, our shopping centers, our movies, and our churches will continue to flood with human blood.

If you take weapons away from man, he will no longer rule over the animal kingdom, nor over himself. Instead, he will learn to be himself, rather than something he has become due to his imaginary boundaries – a coward and killer!

I am puzzled by political and religious society members who favor to hunt and kill animals. Allowing themselves permission to kill nature for sport. Yet they expect for gang members and other violent figures, who live in concrete jungles, such as the projects and barrios to suddenly stop the violence and drop their weapons. Can you not see that they are the reason they have these weapons to begin with. Much like the terrorist we supply and train, or like the cartels we arm, we create these monsters.

It is not difficult at all to purchase guns legally or illegally in America. It is no secret that guns can be purchased anywhere, anytime by anyone in our Country. Every single night on the news, man is being broadcasted for shooting his or her fellow humans. Some kill out of self-defense and others kill with intentions. Regardless of what, these individuals have chosen to kill, and, in several cases, many will get away with it.

It has been said that history repeats itself, in the case of war; man has killed millions and has been honored for it continuously. America, renowned as perhaps the most powerful nation of all nations, has killed countless lives; yet no solider will go to prison for taking someone's life, but that does not mean that they are free.

Such individuals will suffer mentally from the anguish of not listening to their common sense. PTSD and depression are real; they are real because we have betrayed nature and our common sense. Since 9/11, way over 30,000 soldiers have died by committing suicide.

In the bible, the authors order God's people to murder certain individuals and/or societies numerous times. To command any human to kill and to follow through on such ignorance is to fall short of using one's common sense. If political and military officials demand you to kill thy enemy, they have failed to understand that there is no enemy. There are only the divisions in our mind, known as imaginary boundaries.

No country has the authority to recruit and send innocent young adults to war. War produces killers who will suffer greatly from regret and mental depression. We are sending our precious youth down this path, when as many as 500,000 troops who served in the middle east wars have been diagnosed with PTSD.

And even though the diagnosis name PTSD was not adopted until the late 70's, over 700,000 soldiers suffered from PTSD when they returned home from the Vietnam war and this true for any and every war worldwide. It's time to stop, we cannot keep doing this to our fellow human beings, especially to our youth on both sides of the coin.

As blinding as it may seem; the criminal who kills or the soldier who fights for his country, and/or the police officer who murders, are of no difference in the eyes of nature. They have killed and all who do must pay the price of Karma. Those who slip through the cracks of manmade laws and learn forgive themselves for doing so, simply because the political and religious societies say it is ok, are those who are most susceptible to bad karma in future lifetimes.

Many humans have been mass-murders in disguise and even though many have gotten away with it; no human can escape the laws of nature and karma. Nature does not allow humans wearing certain uniforms (military and police) to kill people and get away with it. It is people blinded by their imaginary boundaries that allow themselves to think this way. They put themselves into these situations by engaging in the struggles for unauthentic power. I hear our so-called leaders claiming we need to put more guns into the hands of "the good guys", at any time a so-called "good guy" with a gun can snap and become influenced by his negative emotions.

Here's the reality, a person can choose to do good and bad in his or her lifetime, so we cannot distinguish if a person is good or bad, but we can do is <u>limit</u> them to having *access* to guns. Here is the most common one that ignorant people will use, guns don't shoot people, people shoot people. Every debate is centered around those words. Sadly, you cannot win against this immature mindset because their imaginary boundaries block them from recognizing this simple fact. It's not the guns that kill people, they're absolutely correct; it's blinded, witless people who have <u>*Access*</u> to guns that kill people!

Take the story of Kyle Rittenhouse, the 17-year-old who killed two people and injured one. He had no business being out there at those riots with guns intended for war, yet he murdered two lives and got away with it. He got away with it through the laws of man, but not by the laws of nature. This young man will suffer from mental anguish, karma, and harassment for the rest of his life, because what he did was wrong!

If we are to ever have heaven on earth, we must delete from this planet that which is not safe for humanity, like weapon manufacturers whose sole purpose is creating means of us murdering each other. Without these weapons in America, humans can become what the creator created them to be, and not the cowards they have become.

I know it will hurt many feelings out there, especially those on the right, because they feel that it is there God given right, but if given the choice to bring back all of the millions of victims (especially the children) that we have lost due to gun violence or to put into place a law that hurts your feelings by banning guns, I would choose hurting people's feelings any day. Humans do not need guns to survive, they just think they do.

How many more people must we lose in order to gain control over the weapons that are clearly killing us? How can we create a world of peace and harmony; a life in search of life, liberty, and the pursuit of happiness in a world where we are dodging bullets? Who will take control of this madness if we do not, here and now? Please use your common sense to answer these significant questions and then speak out! Remember it is your money and thoughts that control all of this.

Unlike those blinded by the imaginary boundaries of their mind, this book was written in hopes of interpreting the laws of nature in the most comprehensible manner. If through these pages I become known as rebellious, then so be it, because one of the most important objectives Americans must do now, is to ensure a safe future and stand strong; not for our race, religion, or color of skin, but for all of humanity! History will repeat itself, until we can learn from it, and decide to change it.

Unfortunately, history cannot repeat itself if we destroy the earth with mass destructive weapons and/or through global warming, nor can we bring back the countless victims that have already died due to firearms. History does not give back life to those countless lives lost to diseases, illnesses, and viruses.

What history does provide for humanity is the knowledge to gain control over the bad habits that we have persistently accumulated since the existence of humankind, such as all the callousness that has manifested by minds blinded by imaginary boundaries. If we can learn to acknowledge and conquer those bad habits, then humanity will survive and become stronger and closer than any other species to ever exist.

Born into a world of the unknown, humans have progressed into a world they now own. One continuous awful habit humans are faced with is the desire to control others. Slavery, the oppression of woman, and cruelty to gays and trans people are all prime examples of the desire to control others. Each of these acts can be found in the first testament of the bible.

The authors often infuse the word of the lord with their own intentions and these authors unknowingly have shaped a modern world of hate and disconnection due to their own imaginary boundaries (their own blindness). Today, fortunately through our acceptance of our commons sense; slaves, women and homosexuals are breaking through this ill creed and are living proof that not all that is written in the holy scriptures is righteous or even the word of God!

In God's eye's we are all his children. A God created through imaginary boundaries will divide it's children; which the bible has been doing for millenniums. A God who supposedly orders you to control, torture, kill and/or rape any other human is actually a man in his struggle for power. This society and the political society will forever battle for unauthentic power, for each was founded on such principles. In order to disengage from the power struggles of life, we must learn to follow the scriptures that are permanently written within, because those are the universal law's that come to us through our common sense.

We must rediscover our common connection to one another and learn to see the beauty in all things, especially the beauty in Nature. Trust in the universe that all is well and will be well. Visualizing rather than mere hoping or praying is an essential law of nature. To visualize is to manifest and crystallize what you desire into physical reality. Those who have been oppressed by the holy scriptures and other likeminded creeds, visualized a time when they would be free, that time has come, right here, right now.

As we keep pushing forward, we know within what is right and what is wrong. Yet right now in America, we still have racism in our country. Why? Maybe because we have politicians wanting to make America great again, with their hidden agendas, trying to send us back into segregation and division, but minorities are no longer tolerating the intolerance and discriminatory ways of the past. They are now standing up for themselves and coming together and fighting for their freedoms.

-Daze of Discovery-

The land known as the America was said to be discovered by bible believers, thus, we have become a nation under God. When Christopher Columbus discovered America, he had merely discovered a thriving land already owned and occupied. However not by God's people, but people who closely resembled the description of Jesus himself.

Immediately settlers granted themselves and their societies the power over those of a different language, culture, and belief. Blinded by the imaginary boundaries in their mind that came with them from overseas, they began their quest for unauthentic power and attempted to convert the natives into Christianity. Those that did not want to be converted became slaves or exiled.

Settler's began pushing Natives into lands that they did not want and herding them into pockets of reservations, generating treaties that stood for nothing, because they would be broken by America. Natives did not ask immigrants for a multitude of documents to come into this country "legally" - They were humble and one with nature and did not realize their kind (people of color) were being overthrown by white Christian ideology.

In one particular case, Columbus accused the Indians of stealing clothing from the Spaniards. Columbus, (Mr. Love thy Neighbor) grabbed a native and sliced his ear off. This sparked the gruesome annihilation of the Native inhabitants, which would ultimately become all but nearly erased, like the buffalo. The land and nature which was once home to the Native Indians, who loved and lived as one with nature would ultimately become no different than the land in which settlers we're trying to escape from. A land flooded with laws, rules, creeds, racism and bloodshed.

American grounds began to flood with the blood and demise of the Great American Indian race and culture. Near the death of Columbus, he insisted that he had a God given right to govern all the lands in which he discovered. Giving proof that bible believers throughout history and into the future will always feel superior towards those who live without the influence of this imaginary boundaries mindset and religious beliefs. Another words, Christianity cannot live in peace with others of a different belief system or mindset, without trying to convert or dissolve them.

Yet, another form of intolerance from a religious perspective or from this society comes from none other than Archbishop Ussher of Ireland. He and his followers thoroughly studied the scriptures and strongly concluded that God created the earth on Sunday, October 23, 4004 B.C. Of course, geologist later revealed a more accurate account, dating the earth back 4.5 billion years. I'm sure Ussher and his team calculated correctly according to the scriptures and the book of Genesis. However according to evolution and reality, he was only off by a few billion years.

Blinded by the imaginary boundaries that limit our imagination, Ussher also proclaimed that dinosaur fossils discovered were depicted as devices planted by the devil to delude man. As a result, these "devil devices" stand tall in museums worldwide to remind humanity that they too, can be extinct off the face of earth.

Learn from the dinosaur that roamed on mother earth for more than 100 million years without polluting it or abusing it. Nature, which already existed for billions of years, prior to Moses's so-called creations of heaven and earth. It was not just Moses to get it incorrect, for example, ancient Egyptians believed that the universe was an enormous room; the earth was its floor, the sky, a vast ceiling supported on four great columns and hung nightly by the gods with lamps of stars. Of course, we now know that this is untrue, but every culture, religion and/or region has its own story of creation. They are just theories that helped humans of the past understand life and where they thought we came from.

Through the course of time scientist have discovered that the earth that we live on is but a minor satellite of a second-rate star on the outer fringe of our galaxy, the Milky Way. And as our solar system is to the Milky Way, so the Milky Way is to the galaxies of outer space... Infinite. Today, it is known that there are over 100 billion stars in our galaxy and our galaxy is only one of 100 billion galaxies in the universe.

Our planet earth is in a position sustained within our solar system, just as nature is confined by the ozone layer, just as our souls are held within the human body; which is all connected to the intangible force we refer to as – gravity. Isacc Newton helped discover and explain gravity to humanity. Columbus was aware of this force, when and his crew bravely sailed off to the far sides of earth, "discovering" unknown lands.

Earth is the only known planet in our solar system to offer and sustain life. Most of earth's life comes from the areas closest to the equator. The sun, the water and land produce life, if you take any of these three away, life as we know it will forever be changed. The Sun is the most significant star in our universe because it brings light, warmth, and life to this planet.

Understand that there is only one earth within our reach; it is unique because it is capable of producing nature – us! Nature is beautiful when it is appreciated from within or seen from outer space; far too often, innocent minds are taught to believe that the earth is evil or that we are merely passing through on our search for salvation, that is nonsense. If you listen to your common sense, life on earth can be a wonderful experience, if you don't, a life blinded by imaginary boundaries can be hell.

You have a choice right now to begin to view all things true and from within or continue to be blinded. The earth offers salvation for those who claim it. Only time stands between saving and destroying this beautiful planet and our human race. Future generations need not live by the fear of weapons, nor by the torments of imaginary boundaries; but instead, by the love of nature. Only then are we truly empowered.

The tree which moves
some to tears of joy is in the
eyes of others only a green thing
which stands in the way.
Some see nature all ridicule
and deformity, and by these
I shall not regulate
my propositions.
And some see no nature
at all. But to the eyes of the
man of imagination,
Nature is imagination itself.

-William Blake

-<u>Herd Expectancy</u>-

All around the world, herds are gathering and forming churches, sects, cults, and new religions. They believe that the son of God will be returning soon; he and his heavenly forces will than destroy the cruel, warmongering, antichrist, and evilness of this world and ultimately, he will than set up his ever-lasting kingdom. More than 60% of 332 million Americans believe that this will one day occur. Christianity is the largest religion in the world with an estimated 2.4 billion members worldwide.

There are many Gods and many religions throughout the world. What makes America unique is that at the time when the declaration of independence and the constitution were written, the founding fathers did not intend to create a nation based exclusively on the principles of Christianity. Instead, they wanted to ensure that we would *not* fall to the domination of any one religion or faith.

So, they wrote in the very first sentence of the first Amendment in the US Constitution, "Congress shall make no law respecting an establishment of religion" meaning that the government cannot take away individual rights of religion. It also means that no state or government can set up a church and tell you how you need to believe. Separation of State and Church is what our founding fathers intended to do because it protects a government from imposing one religion over another. Which is what many people in congress are trying to do nowadays, they want to bring their religion into politics.

The Christian Faith was built around one man, a man like no other, for he was said to have possessed the actual key (attributes) which unlocks the door to peace and heaven on earth. The key is no great mystery or secret; we each possess the key inside because the key is and will forever be – <u>LOVE</u>!

Love has always been the answer, yet we dwell in the things that divide us. I have seen so many variants of the Christian faiths that proclaim they truly believe in Jesus and his powerful message to love one another as he has loved us, yet they fight and kill over their petty differences. Any religion or pastor that degrades another religion, is not loving all and especially his neighbor, therefore, they are spreading division and not divinity in the name of Jesus.

How could someone whom the new world beholds as the <u>only</u> son of God despise not only the first testament (the knowledge of his co-called father) but also the religion in which flourished from his knowledge. How? Jesus died escaping the strains he was born into. The imaginary boundaries of his time; namely, religion. Yet he wouldn't have, had he known that though his sacrifice would emerge an even greater society blinded by imaginary boundaries bearing his last name and doing the exact same things that the Jews did in his time.

What Jesus taught was unlike the religions of his time; most religious leaders hated and envied Jesus, for he taught about the greatest truth of all, LOVE! He transcended the most significant law of nature, the more you love the more love you receive. The energy you put out to the universe, is the energy that will come back to you. Jesus really understood nature and was close to nature and used it to teach valuable lessons through his parables on nature. He was one with nature.

Jesus instructed us to love one another, and to love our neighbors, which means to love everyone and to do all things through love. Jesus taught his followers to think freely from the imaginary boundaries that gripped the minds of those that were being controlled, much like today. If Jesus were alive today, he would be so saddened over what has erroneously manifested through his death.

Jesus did *not* die for your sins, he died because the leaders of his time were furious over the freedom he was prophesying about. The things he could see were beyond what a mind blinded by imaginary boundaries could see. This is the real reason why Jesus died, because he tried freeing the masses from control and those that are blinded do not want people to be free, because then they cannot be herded.

Religious and Political leaders of his time grew furious and jealous of Jesus, for they knew, he was unblinding the herds from the authority those leaders yearned for, much like today. This is why the Jewish leaders went to the Romans for help. His teaching in the darkest of times brought light and involved love, kindness, and equality for all, the total opposite of what is written in the first testament. That was way too much to handle in those days for the narrow minded; eventually they became envious and hypocritical; Jesus was arrested, condemned, and crucified by both the religious and political societies of his day.

Jesus wanted no ties with religion, yet humanity has found every way possible to tie his last name to the second testament and the countless Christian Faiths that have been manifested into our reality. Creating limitless Christian variants who constantly fight to be correct and represent the absolute truth.

Paul Kurt is Author of "<u>FORBIDDEN FRUIT</u>" and writes "Humans have been ingenious in inventing an infinite variety of belief systems that enable us to cope with the problems encountered in living…But to think that everything on this minor planet and in the total universe was created for man is to inflate our egos."

It is this egotistical way of thinking which has led man to abuse and misuse nature. This way of thinking has blinded humanity into cutting down most of our forest, which has led to the extinction of countless species of plants and animals. It has led him to destroy and taint the land, the water, and the air we breathe. This way of thinking is why the entire planet sits on death row now, with a date much closer than you can imagine.

While countless individuals are busy earning a one-way ticket into heaven, he or she is neglecting to do all that he or she can for the earth, humanity, and especially for future generations. Often, we are taught that we are merely passing through on our way to a fictional salvation, where we will live forever or dwell in hell forever. We are taught that the earth belongs to "the Devil" and that we born evil.

By comparing the signs written in the book of revelations, to the catastrophes that mankind has caused, is to grant ignorant people permission to continue destroying earth. To blame all of this on the enemy, such as the devil is to fail to understand that all of this is due to the thoughts of man. We inherited a pristine planet, and everyone should try their best to leave it better than they found it; not just pass though.

Since the beginning of time, (human time) man's ego has driven him to want to be ruler of all things. Even in modern times exists a hierarchy stature in every entity of life. The desire to be master of everything and reign above all has caused humanity terrible pain and suffering. When all we had to do, all along was learn to master our own thoughts. This is the process of mastering your domain and securing your destiny and truly being at peace with everyone.

If you have read the first testament you will find why Jesus was against this literature. It is because it does <u>not</u> teach of a God who is all loving. To assure of this, in Exodus 32:27 God commands Israelites "put every man his sword by his side and go in and out from gate throughout the camp and slay every man." As a result, thousands were murdered.

Mr. Kurtz points out that "In the Ten Commandments (Exodus, 20:14): God says, "though shall not commit adultery". Yet after commanding the Hebrew conquering army to kill all Midianite captives, including innocent woman and children, God permit's the army (including married men) to seize and keep the young virgins for themselves:" "But all the women _children_, that have not known a man by lying with him, keep alive for yourselves." (num. 31:18)

Please tell me, if this is truly a God or merely a man giving himself permission to take and rape underage minors? Just take a moment to think about this. Think of our leaders today, if they were to command our military do the exact same thing now, how many of you would be ok with this command? Would you just agree and say, it's God's word, its ok to do it because he said so. Please use your common sense to answer these questions. The bible is full of these types of commands from "God".

As you can see, this God which Moses invented has caused endless suffering, pain, and countless deaths. Clearly this is a God invented by the finite mind of man in hopes of over-powering others. The authors of the bible were ingenious to intertwine fantasy and reality, and many were able to extract some of the laws of nature and universal truths from their creative imagination; however, we must accept that this literature was intended for their time and not ours. Read the bible for yourself, everything in there is, he said, she said and often written decades if not centuries after the stories were told.

Is there truth and valuable lessons in the bible, yes of course there are some, as with most religions around the world; the literature is intended to be a moral compass guideline of how humans should behave. There are truths to all religions but there also numerous things that are truly man's ego and unjust in all the scriptures of all religions, because they are written by humans, humans blinded by imaginary boundaries. I know that this is hard to digest, but it is the truth, these authors are merely humans.

In short, you can thank these authors for dispersing throughout humanity the seeds of; prostitution, rape, sexual abuse, sexual abuse to minors, incest, oppression, hostility, murder, war, and slavery, just to name a few. Understand that God is not authorizing and commanding such heinous crimes, humans are.

Please do not become offended in anyway, simply attempt to read the bible for yourself with no one interpreting it and I do mean the first testament, and you shall find these, and even more disturbing realisms created by man posing as God. Take for instance, in Exodus 21:20-21, it originally reads: "Anyone who beats their male or female slave with a rod must be punished, if the slave dies as a direct result, 21 but they are not to be punished if the slave recovers after a day or two, since the slave is their property."

Of course, it has evolved through interpretation now so that humans can think that the bible is abolishing slavery, but it is clear, that these authors were pro-slavery and promoted possessing humans as mere property.

Here is the watered down, all loving translated version that can be found Google search: "If a man strikes his male servant or his female servant with a staff so that he or she dies as a result of the blow, he will surely be punished." (Exodus 21:20, NET)." They continue; "This command again abolishes slavery and it's abuses. No one is allowed to beat another to death. If someone works for you, they are not your property." Yet the real verbiage says they are your property and as long as you don't beat them to death then you're ok.

See how they flip the words of this atrocity? To begin with the original texts were written in a language we cannot understand, converted with the intentions to display what the interpreters wanted to display and transmuted to keep this dogma holier than thou. Then religious leaders pick only the good from such erratic scriptures and present only love and kindness and translate it in such a way as to blind you, as they are unknowingly blinded themselves.

Even in the New Testament, in Peter 2:18 "Slaves, be subject to your masters with all reverence, not only to those who are good and gentle, but also to those who are perverse." Of course, nowadays the word perverse has been changed to unjust or cruel.

It's strange that evolution is so hard for Christians to believe in, yet the verbiage in the bible seems to always be evolving into the most kind and generous interpretations. Both the first and second testament never suggest to NOT own slaves or even attempt to free slaves, instead they teach slaves and slave owners how to treat each other, but never do either of the bible's authors say that slavery is wrong. Humanity has had to overcome this harsh reality, defiantly going against the teachings of the scriptures.

Attend various religious services and you will discover the many patterns of tone used to distinguish them vary. Just as an auctioneer or a news caster, each religion variant has adopted patterns of tone themselves. Bearing evidence that these are taught patterns; they are taught to accumulate money from those willing to pay to be taught about something that is omnipresent and free - spirituality. These imaginary bound societies that we call religions also exist today only because of the people's money and their inability to see beyond imaginary boundaries.

Not all religions are based upon accumulating riches; some are doing good things to help the less fortunate, immigrants, those addicted to drugs and those who just need guidance. And I send my blessing to all those ministries that are doing what Jesus would do. Although, all religions are inconclusive and have originated by minds blinded by imaginary boundaries. What we are witnessing today is the evolution of God and church and now more than ever God, church, and politics intertwined.

Please read carefully because this may be the most important piece of wisdom that I can share with you in this literature. To connect with the Devine, you do not need greedy religious leaders rendering their interpretation of the bible for a one-way ticket into heaven. All the answers already thrive within you and at any time the divine is ever so present. God is not written in the pages of some books written thousands of years ago; God is written within your soul.

The Dilemma we are faced with since the beginning of our time, is we have forgotten where we come from and more importantly, who we come from. This is the knowledge that religious and political leaders do not want you to know about, because this knowledge leads to the freedom of the enslaved mind; this knowledge will set you free!

- <u>The Creation</u> -

We are living in a world governed by opinions. Some opinions became laws, while others became beliefs. An example of these opinions is shared by bible believers worldwide over the creations of earth and mankind. Here is a theory that was written in the bible and is proclaimed to be the absolute truth of how we came into being.

In the beginning God created the heavens and earth, the animal kingdom; eventually, all of nature and by the sixth day God made man in his *own* image. The lord formed man out of the dust of the ground and breathed into him, life, and man became a living being. God then cast man to sleep and surgically removes one of his ribs and magically transforms a woman out of it (this was the beginning of degrading woman) and calls her Eve. Ironically, Adam's surgery went well, and he lived a healthy long life until his 930th birthday. Impotence was no problem for Adam, because he became a father at the tender age of 130 years old and from these two emerged all of humanity to reign over all of nature.

Again, all of the answers are deep within you. But just think about this for a moment, does this sound fictional to you in any way? Is this how we truly came into being? Couldn't the authors have chosen God to create a woman, when he created man; rather than degrading woman and claiming she came from a rib of a man. A man that was supposedly made in the image of the lord of the universe.

Here is the reality, we are not formed in God's image, but we did come from God's imagination, as did everything else in the universe and that is because God is shapeless and omnipresent. Most religions agree that the creator is not some old man in heaven, but God is however the greatest intangible energy to ever exist – the infinite intangible spirit. There are many names for GOD; the universal mind, Buddha, Allah, Infinite intelligence, Jehovah, the creator, etc. and none are wrong.

You can call God whatever you'd like or describe God however you'd like, but the God that is written in one book isn't any better than a God written in another book. God is formless, God is light, God is pure energy and ultimately the Great Spirit or grand intangible energy that we all come from, but we are <u>NOT</u> made in his image!

All religions can agree in our time that God is love, yet all religions can hate; because all religions and their text we're founded by the finite mind. Such scriptures are divinely inspired but not written by divine intelligence. This is why, rather than celebrating our love for God, we will kill, debate, try to convert and just cause misery in the essence of our creator. God did not just have one son, we are all God's children, every single one of us.

The source created us to utilize every one of us, to experience life through us. Once you realize this universal truth, you will be able to accept everyone for who they are, regardless of how they are, the way Jesus Christ did in his lifetime. This Prayer is so profound and one of my favorites, because ultimately, we are instruments of God and God is working through all of us to make this wonderful vibration, we call life.

Lord, make me an instrument of your peace:
where there is hatred, let me sow love;
where there is injury, pardon;
where there is doubt, faith;
where there is despair, hope;
where there is darkness, light;
where there is sadness, joy.
O divine Master, grant that I may not so much seek
to be consoled as to console,
to be understood as to understand,
to be loved as to love.
For it is in giving that we receive,
it is in pardoning that we are pardoned,
and it is in dying that we are born to eternal life.

- St. Francis of Assisi

(38)

-The Fear of Death-

Why is that we fear death so much? Perhaps it is all the confusion and mis-understanding that is stigmatized with death. Our world has adopted three after death scenarios. One of which produces fear throughout entire lifetimes and is brought to you by none other than the same authors of creation. Most bible believers stake their version of the afterlife as eternity in heaven or hell. Others, like the Buddhist believe that when a person dies, he or she simply enters a state of nirvana, or a long eternal sleep.

The third version of after death was grasped by Plato. Plato was a well-known Greek Philosopher who left the first writings on human intellect and on knowing thy-self. A pioneer in expanding consciousness to say the least. Plato picked up on something way before his time, mainly because he was so connected to his inner voice, his common sense. Plato brought to our consciousness the concept of reincarnation, also shared by Hindus and many Buddhists worldwide. Even some of our Jewish brothers spoke of reincarnation in the time of Jesus and as hard as this may be for some to believe, it is estimated that around 25% to 30% of Americans that are Christians today believe in reincarnation.

Still the religious theory of after-life is what most Americans have been taught to believe in, in order to preserve the stories of the bible. In the original bible you will find that Moses killed an Egyptian and tried to bury him without being seen. God who sees everything and senses all, made Moses well aware of his actions, through regret and sorrow or in reality, through his subconscious mind. God did _not_ come to Moses as a burning bush to write the Ten Commandments, Moses understood "Thou shall not kill" because he had already killed and tried to get away with it and could not take it anymore.

Moses knew he was wrong because of his common sense and because of his feelings of regret and sorrow. Ultimately the creative mind of Moses shaped a God in his image that would forgive him and help clear his conscious mind after committing such sin. You will never hear someone acknowledging on Sunday morning, that Moses killed, then said "though shall not kill", then ordered thousands to be killed, but that is exactly what he did. Moses; was perhaps the most cunning mass murderer of all time, for from the mind of serial killer arose "the God", and from that God, emerged Judaism,

Christianity, and the Muslim religions. A God that still reigns in American culture today and proof of how easy humans can be tricked into believing anything. Moses was a man who got away with murder, and he is still getting away with murder now! He's just killing them nowadays with blindness.

Now please do not get me wrong, my intensions are *not* to destroy the bible, (that will happen on its own) it's just to bring light to the fact that the bible was written by people, for people that were struggling for freedom in their time. It was written not so that we take everything literally thousands of years later, but so that we take what resonates and use it to move forward based off of our common sense. This is the greatest truth about the bible, not all that is written in the bible is truth.

I myself am a devout believer in the way Christ lived and loved. So please understand that I am not trying to destroy any religion, I am trying to get all religions and even those who are not religious to understand that we are all one and not any one religion is the only way or is the absolute truth, those that argue that, are those most unlike Christ.

You see, all religions have truth to them, mixed with fallacy; therefor they cannot be the absolute truth. Religions are good in keeping tradition alive and it works for many because they bring into the subconscious mind emotions such as love, hope, and peace. The universe responds to the energy you put out. What you give, you shall receive. What you think, you shall become, and those are laws of nature. So, in a sense it exercises the mind's capabilities, and another believer is born. I know religion is helpful to many around the world because it offers structure and helps invoke positive energy to the subconscious mind, which in turn produces positive outcomes in life. This can be seen as being "born again" or "seeing the light" or being "baptized," but in reality, it's just a shift in our consciousness, which we will cover in another chapter.

This is extremely important to the soul of every human being. For those of you currently active in any religious societies/churches, your heart is the right place, because you are seeking spiritual growth. However, keep in mind that true Spiritual Growth comes from within and only within can one attain the Devine. Mathew 6:6, Jesus said, "But when you pray, go into your room, and shut the door and pray to your Father who is in secret. And your father who sees in secret will reward you."

There are three main ways to acquire spiritual growth; one is when you go within and connect with the divine, through exercises such as prayer, meditation, Reiki, Ta chi, Yoga, Qi Gong, etc. The other happens, quite simply, when you are in the presence or submerged in the beauty of Nature. Both can recharge your soul's batteries because you are connected to spirit in both. The third is when we are connected to your *purpose* or calling through your creative imagination; when you're "in the zone." This could be in a recording studio for a singer or on a canvas for a painter or on a court or field for an athlete.

Do not blind yourselves into thinking that love and happiness can only be obtained during religious functions. Happiness is a choice; it is a state of being. Jesus knew this, therefore he, unlike those that teach about him went out to the people, rather than building a power-hungry service or a mega church.

He didn't attempt to convert or devise a creed that would form a religion. People after his death did that and are still doing it today. He never preached or taught any complicated ceremonies or difficult rules. All he did was show love!

The only thing that Jesus attempted to destroy was the organized religion of his time. Jesus grew God-like, in that he loved and treated everyone equally. He saw life without all the imaginary boundaries that were planted in hm, which was a miracle within itself, because most cannot do this. In fact, this was probably his greatest miracle. For some-one to have such auspicious visions in the darkest of ages is what made Jesus truly special; but even Jesus said anyone amongst you could do the things that I've done and even greater things. Meaning he was an exceptional human being with tremendous faith and love for all; and also, a profound understanding and compassion for nature. And you are no different because we are all capable of being God-like, because God is within us each of us.

From "<u>Everyday Wisdom</u>" Dr. Wayne W. Dyer writes "If you are going to follow your bliss and make a difference in the world, you will soon learn you cannot follow the heard. Rather than put a label on yourself as a Christian, Jew, Muslim, Buddhist or whatever, instead make a commitment to be Christ-like, God-like, Budda-like, Mohammed-like. Rather than being against evil, be only for love".

Many religious and political leaders talk about these greats around the world yet are nothing like them. Love dissolves all imaginary boundaries; love does not favor war or acts of violence and hate crimes. Love does not judge, envy, or allow humans to be hypocritical. Love all things unconditionally, including yourself and you too can be God-like.

One who truly loves life is not searching for the end of time or to die. The infamous cults in which have committed mass suicide are mostly sects of extreme bible believers. Meaning they take every word that is written in the bible literally as do most bible believers, and in 1997 Americans saw firsthand what this extremist mindset can do to a human mind, when we witnessed 39 active members of the Heaven's Gate commit mass suicide. Bearing evidence that the imagination of heaven and hell becomes so real to such individuals; that he or she is blinded from reality; so, blinded that humans can be coerced into committing suicide or accepting sin as God's will.

These cult leaders live out their interpretation of the bible and blind their members by forming these minor, secular societies that believe they are separate or superior to the rest of humanity. These movements are happening right now in Christian churches all around the world, much like Warren Jeff's and David Koresh who read the pages of the bible and believed that their God was ok with polygamy and child sexual abuse. It is men like this that use the bible to brainwash the weak and instill fear in them.

Take for example the story of the mega church movement – La Luz del Mundo (light of the world) Three generation spanning back to the 1920's, of insane sexual abuse, and it's members still believe that their leaders are living Gods till this day. This is being brainwashed in the name of religion or blinded by faith and sadly it won't ever stop, until we can accept and see passed imaginary boundaries.

Most of these bible believers desire the end because it brings God. Their love for death becomes greater than their love for life. This is known as the fear of death and for many this can be the cruelest of all human fears. Most cannot see it, but when we pray to God continuously, yearning to live an eternal life in heaven, heaven and for that matter hell are unknow to humans. Hence, we fear what we do not know. This sets up the fear of death because a person who prays a lifetime to enter the kingdom of God is praying in hopes that he or she does not end up in hell. The thought of eternal punishment can cause a lifetime of fear, but here is the real fear we must worry about.

If we go into a nuclear war or continue to be careless with mother nature and not take global warming seriously, we will dwell in a world that will transit into a hell-like state. No one on earth will be exempt from this horror of transitions. Life will not end per se, but our world will transition into a hot, desolate planet; a planet much like the hell that many religions are unknowingly visualizing us into. We will become un-human like creatures adapting to the most negative of chemicals ever composed and/or we will have to restore from the ground up after these mega-storms become so enraged that all is lost and reset. We will lose the beauty of life, nature and all the auspicious visions we carry within us.

Is this really the kind of world that we want to leave behind? I am going to ask you to sincerely dispel the fear of death, which has gripped the minds of humans, all throughout history. Learn and trust from the specialized knowledge of science and other related fields that have shed light on discoveries needed to release this fear. This is exclusive knowledge that needs to be taught to everyone, because this is significant to our existence.

Napoleon Hill teaches the process for which reincarnation is no longer a question but a fact. "The entire world is made up of only two things, energy, and matter. In elementary physics we learn that neither matter nor energy (the only two realities known to man) can be created or destroyed. Both matter and energy can be transformed but neither can be destroyed, of course, life cannot be destroyed. Life, like other forms of energy, may be passed through various processes of transition, or change, but it cannot be destroyed. Death is mere transition. If death is not mere change, or transition, then nothing comes after death except a long, eternal, and peaceful sleep, and sleep is nothing to be feared. Thus, you may wipe out, forever, the fear of death."

The fear of death is merely a state of mind. Understand that it is your soul that breathes life into our biological bodies, and it is your soul that is an infinite energy pattern and thus, a product of continuous and beautiful reincarnations, as you will learn in the following chapter.

(43)

-The Infinite Soul-

The truth is humans have always wished upon the stars to live one life forever here on earth. The desire to be immortal has been a dream to virtually every human being. Those who take their life do so, not because they wanted to, but because they cannot escape the wrath of imaginary boundaries placed upon them by society. The pressure is unbearable and unfair because the human mind, body, and soul, just wants to be free and loved.

The authors of the bible have proposed an eternal life in heaven or hell. Even most of Moses' characters lived well pasted eight centuries before entering their eternal life. Scientists have searched endlessly for the fountain of youth, to slow or surrender the natural aging process. When in truth, we must learn to accept that we are a perpetual, endless, pattern of this universe. We are an eternal energy pattern vibrating at what is human consciousness.

Author Aldous Huxley once stated; "When the doors of perception are cleansed, man will see things as they truly are, infinite." Thus, acknowledge and accept the infinite soul. The very soul that permits you to simultaneously intake this very sentence and breath of fresh air. The human body will die; yet the soul will continue its eternal course, indefinitely. Over the years, we have made the soul a complex issue, when in fact, the soul is simple, because it is pure energy. Souls are intangible forms of energy derived from the infinite energy.

Through nature, the energy within you has existed though countless of beings and will continue to exist long after your body is gone. Most are unaware of this, for with each beginning, brings forth a new body, mind, setting, and life. Some can retain knowledge from a passed life, but those blinded by imaginary boundaries will not give them credit, because it goes against what they have been taught to believe.

When one dies, the soul will have a review or reflection period with infinite intelligence. In this process your soul will be completely submerged with the energy that created. Here is the reality of what happens when a human body passes away. Whatever you believe will happen - will happen. Meaning if you believe you're going to heaven, you will dwell in a heavenly afterlife; if you believe or fear in hell or

(44)

Purgatory than that is what you will experience. The good news is, that it is not our forever home, it is not where you will spend eternity, it is our intangible home, but we are merely passing through on our way to being born again. These are the laws of nature.

You can dwell in infinite intelligence as long as needed, but eventually you will have to manifest into being born again, because God created us this way, so that God can experience love and life through our existence. We had it wrong this whole time; God did create everything in this universe for man. God created humans, so that God could experience the universe through humans, and God does this with every other living creature and organism as well, God lives vicariously through all lifeforms.

The transition to being reborn can take some time or it can be instant. What I mean is when you are dying in this life and your loved ones are saying their goodbyes here, you can be transitioning to a new family and they can be welcoming you there, at birth. The soul is energy; therefore, it has no vision; a soul does not recognize race, religion, male or female, etc. The spirit is in search of life; to transit the energy that it is, (human) into a new being that best resounds with its souls purpose and personality. This is the circle of life, it has no end and no beginning, it just continuously flows.

As soon as we are born, the awakening process begins. Slowly we develop our consciousness. We become familiar with our new body and settings. Our memory and intuition come into play during our adolescence. We learn the language of the land, the customs of the culture, the taste of the foods, and ultimately, you learn, the new you!

As children we glare up at vast blue skies, perhaps in our play pen or at a park and we know that we are alive again. We recognize colors, shapes, scents, and feelings that remind us of past existences, because the human senses are emerging within us as well. Common sense develops within us and suddenly we know within, what is dangerous to us and what can kill us.

Unfortunately, imaginary boundaries are taught, and they do not validate these realities and humans slowly <u>lose</u> their inner connection to the prime energy source of the soul, and sadly, to each other. This then leads to the struggle for power and a highly destructive world of violence and ignorance, we begin preying on each other.

The kingdom of Heaven is right here on earth, this is our everlasting kingdom. Look around because we are making it a hell very quickly. But it does not have to be this way; we just need to fully *awaken* now and remember these hidden truths before it is too late again. I say again, because our souls have already been through this quandary many times over in our 14-billion-year journey; we have lived, always trying to get it right, then we become our own demise and self-destruct because of our pride, but love is stronger than pride and I hope that we can get it right this time around.

In the Lord's prayer, Jesus taught us to pray like this; he says; "Thy kingdom come; Thy will be done, on earth as it is in heaven." We inherited a breathtaking earth, but we are reckless and clueless species that only cares about "I." Vincent Van Gogh, once stated, "If you truly love nature, you will find beauty everywhere." Opposite of that is if you don't love nature, you will find hell everywhere.

The hell that they are fearing us into, is also becoming a possible reality. We are setting up future existences of hell-like situations for our souls and loved ones in subsequent lives to come. If you really <u>Love</u> your lost ones, you will comprehend that they will return, and what do you want their circumstances to be? What kind of world do you want them to be reborn into? To deny the fact that we are reincarnated is to deny the possibility for a better life each time we are reborn. Another words, we are only hurting ourselves by not caring what happens to the world.

I know that this is a lot to take in, but I also know that when you are reading these hidden truths that have been laid out in these pages, something within you is awakening – It's called the truth with certainty and if we do nothing to ensure our future, at least these fundamentals; life, liberty, and the pursuit of happiness, then we have failed to accept the reality of reincarnation and evolution, the two truths that are indeed absolute.

It is not the Strongest
of the species that survives
not the most intelligent
that survives. It is the one that
is most adaptable to change

Charles Darwin

(46)

-<u>Evolution</u>-

Evolution discredits Moses' theory of creations by billions of years. Obviously, God did not mention to Moses, the great age of Jurassic and cretaceous periods, nor modern day marsupials. Nevertheless, his theory was renowned as a sound concept for thousands of years; that is until Charles Darwin and other scientists shed light and discovered a realistic concept of creation. Mr. Darwin developed his own premise of creation by studying and observing the actual source of life – Nature!

Mr. Darwin's theory became apparent to him on his voyage around the world, specifically to the Galapagos Islands off the coast of South America. Through his discoveries, Charles realized that life begins simple, then evolves into more complex beings. Like a huge tree that sprouts out to the sky, Darwin began to see life in this manner, for each and every species.

Most people debate over the two theories, yet only one is factual. Let us begin with the story of the creation by Moses. After all, it was he who suggested that a God created everything through the process that is now described as intelligent design. This depiction of God breathing life into dust is what evangelicals all across America are fighting for, to be taught in schools, as an alternative to evolution, science and the truth.

At the forefront we have Moses with his ingenious story of how we came into being and the widespread word of theism; then there is his adversary Charles Darwin and his rectifying study titled "<u>THE ORIGIN OF SPECIES</u>." His studies led to the concept of natural selection; meaning those that have adapted and evolved to the circumstances of their surroundings could survive and produce offspring with success.

Although humans are closely related to apes and we share a shocking 98.8 % of their DNA, we did not come from the apes, nor did Charles Darwin contest that we did. Just like an owl did not come from a sparrow, humans did not come from an ape; we derived like an ape, from a prime hominoid call Dryopithecus. This is why our DNA is so close to theirs. This is why there are different types of every species, like for example, different kinds of trees. There are variants of pine, oak, maple and palm trees, to name a few, and even though they are all different, they are all trees. Every species and living organism in nature is like this, for these are the laws of nature.

This concept took the world through an evolutionary spin; suddenly, humanity was presented with an unprecedented depiction of how we came into being and most shockingly, the God that Moses was no longer the creator, nor was the earth, the center of the universe.

In the blink of an eye, the earth was much older than anyone could imagine (4.5 billion years older), and our species could be traced back on its evolutionary journey to 11.1 to 12.5 million years ago. In the process of natural selection, Darwin contended that all species (wild and domestic) diverge from a prime ancestor.

An example would be a species called Moeritherium, it was survived by dinotherium, just like trilophodont was succeeded by Mastodon, who roamed the earth about a million years ago. It gave way in the line of evolution to the great African elephant we know today. Every species has its own evolutionary tree and humans are no exception, we are just taught to believe that we are. The ancestors of Human Beings have been evolving and we are still evolving until this day, evolution never stops.

Our journey started as Dryopithecus, then to Ramapithecus and onto Australopithecus, the first of our ancestors to stand on two legs. Then came the Homo Erectus followed by the homo-sapiens Neanderthalensis, or the Neanderthals. Somewhere around 500,000 years ago, came another significant divergence in our evolutionary chain, like when we slightly divided from the Ape but shared a common ancestor.

Neanderthals were an emotional, skillful, human type of being, who lived side by side with what we once called Cro-Magnon man or the modern human species - us. Both humankinds lived together and learned from one another. Unfortunately, one did not make it, but their DNA can be found all over the human species. Every human being on this planet has some Neanderthal DNA in them, meaning these two species reproduced with one another and advanced are evolutionary benefits.

These humans were sculptors, painters, artists, and family oriented. Before the Neanderthal went extinct, they co-existed with early humans and helped spark modern day civilizations into what have evolved into today, specifically – you!

As we keep searching earth, more and more evidence will be brought to light unveiling the evolutionary chain of humans and those closely related to us. For example, deep within a cave in Africa, scientists and paleontologists recently found another species that emerged alongside humans around 250,000 years ago, Homo Naledi. This was a smaller, more agile relative who stood under five feet and showed signs of gathering in a community setting and displayed emotions like love and caring.

Homo Naledi were unique in that they would crawl into a cave through a tight crawl-space and then into a second chamber, just to bury their loved ones, like an under-ground cemetery. They would take their lost one's through this tumultuous journey deep into the cave and bury them with what tools they had. This discovery was epic because it shows the development of our emotions and awareness of community.

What is really distinctive about them is they looked more ape like and had smaller brains, than modern human beings and the Neanderthals, but they were more like modern humans in that they had a conscious mind and could relate to one another other. It's as if nature was developing the subconscious mind and common sense in that species and is perfecting it in us today.

Evolution, however, goes back even further; from single celled organisms to the complex beings, we have become. Our hominoid tree isn't the beginning of our journey on this planet, for we crawled before we walked and before we crawled, we swam. Missing links in our overall evolutionary journey are popping up everywhere, such as the *Tiktaalik* (the first creature to come out of the water and breathe and walk upon land).

Evolution has brought us to understand the following statement of truth, from which Mr. Hill accurately described how life was created. This is <u>how</u> you and every other living being came into existence: "The earth on which you live, you, yourself, and every other material thing are a result of evolutionary change, through which microscopic bits of matter have been organized and arranged in an orderly fashion. Moreover- and this statement is of stupendous importance – this earth, every one of the billions of individual cells of your body, and every atom of matter, began as an intangible form of energy." When you read this statement, and you use you common sense, you know that this is truth. I don't have to convince you; you just know that it is true.

To complement the statement of truth above, absorb this reality; eloquently worded in Netflix's series, "EARTHSTORM" by narrator Mimi Ndiweni, as she describes the real catalyst to life and evolution. "Ancient volcanoes created life to evolve. Volcanic gases created the atmosphere, which in turn helped create the oceans. And deep underwater hydrothermal vents, volcanic energy powered the chemistry that created the first single-celled organisms and over billions of years, they evolved into us."

This is how we truly became human being and even though you may not remember; your spirit was part of it all. Mother Nature produces life from the materials of this universe; she arranges life in patterns and waves. Take a close look at the palm of your hands and you will see that this statement is true. Each of us is unique in our own patterns, such as lip, finger, and handprints; yet, overall, we belong to the same human pattern. Detectives all over the world have acknowledged this reality of patterns and waves and rely on them when catching their subjects by the uniqueness of their details.

The next time you find yourself mesmerized by the ocean, you will realize that it too is made up of patterns and waves; until you realize, that this stands true for every single living organism in the entire universe, including the universe itself. Understand that this earth is alive and is a part of a living universe that is thriving. Is there life out there? Obviously, because the entire universe is alive and where other stars like our sun our shedding light upon other planets that are positioned in their solar system like earth is to ours, then yes, it's possible. However, these planets are trillions of light years away and we cannot reach them now.

We have evolved through Mother Nature's chemistry into a planet that sustains life. The trees, the animal kingdom and humanity are all but tiny follicles of earth, like our hair is to our head. We are proof that she and every other planet are alive and inner-connected. All energy has a pattern, and every matter takes its form.

Humans have recognized this fact and are now able to send and receive via satellite. televisions, radios, wi-fi and the predictions of weather are all possible now, because we have accepted this reality on a minor level. All of us came from intangible energy manifesting into its physical form, therefore God is in everything and especially within.

To be human is divine, for we are a species that uses its energy unlike all others. With phenomenal brain power, we are finally beginning to understand the intricate matrimony of matter and energy and now more than ever, how to harness this power. Our body configuration combined with our brain power is what makes human-beings capable of being God-like of earth. We are the only pattern of energy that has evolved and can determine the fate of humanity and the fate of the earth.

People who do not believe in evolution are blind to see that our minds alone have evolved greatly in the last 10,000 years. If we listen deep within, through our common sense, you will know that evolution is real because you are part of it. Everything evolves and nothing stays fixed.

On your journey to this moment right now, your soul has witnessed the big bang and the synchronicity of evolution. From the single-celled, non-complex organisms – to the life forms we have become today; evolution is apparent yet sadly, so is our blindness towards it, even when presented with physical evidence, most will deny the truth.

When the dinosaur became extinct, the matter that formed its various bodies transited into new beings of matter. The energy or souls used to power these huge, massive creatures transited into new forms and patterns. This occurs even now, whenever we allow a species to go extinct, it is merely recreated by Mother Nature. When we discover new species, Mother Nature is at hand, doing what she does, creating.

Aids, cancers, and all other deadly diseases are nothing more than reproduced patterns of energy designed by nature. If we can stop ourselves as a whole from erasing thousands of species a year, nature can slow the process of recreating new life forms, many of which can be deadly and non-compatible with humanity. The cure is in this paragraph, how long it takes humanity to comprehend this reality is beyond me.

Understand that the dinosaurs and all the other previous species that are now extinct did not want to go extinct. We, the modern-day animal kingdom, strongly desired to exist. Hence, we are here now and how long we remain is literally for us (humans) to decide. When we as species can grasp the reality of evolution, then we can see our significant role in evolution. Until then, we face global suicide; for we cannot see where we are going, much less believe where we actually come from.

(51)

- **The Creator** -

Through the countless ages of human existence, man has given a flock of opinions to how and when life began, and more importantly, who we came from. Several opinions have been manifested into various belief systems, such as religions. Although times change, one thing will forever remain the same; there are "truths" that humans can believe in and then there are truths with certainty. Understand that beliefs are merely handed over to you, hence they are often received with some doubt, knowing comes from within. William James once stated; "A wise man proportions his belief to the strength of the evidence. Only foolish humans will believe in a proposition for which the evidence is weak or inconclusive."

Understand that the creator of life is not some fanciful, never before seen He, for he is she if anything. Even though most deny her, disrespect her, and abuse her, she remains omnipresent, adoring all of her creations and waiting for us to flow in her direction.

From the perception of all your senses, especially your common sense, you can conceive with a definite certainty that this grand omnipresent divinity exists and flourishes in all and in this moment that we are truly awakening, she will finally receive the praise and the appreciation and love she has longed deserved.

Who is she? Who is the real intelligent designer of all life. She who can bear life of course, the mother of all things real – *Mother Nature!* After reading this chapter and in particular this passage, imaginary boundaries will begin to dissolve, and Imagin to question your taught beliefs. You will visualize, perhaps for the first time, that mother nature is not some made up creed, dogma, or scripture. She does not require some complicated religious system, service or complicated ceremonies to believe in her; simply step outside, she is everywhere, but especially within you. You can see her, you can touch her, you can feel her, you can taste her, you are a part of her, and she is real!

We are living spectacle of the upper most, significant, boundless spirit of energy to ever exist. She is the mother force that composes all creation and sparks life to all intangible entities and components. We have been blessed on earth, to have just the correct elements and matter from the universe and a mother who beautifully arrays life with these elements and moreover, sustains life through evolution.

Combined that with the power of the *Sun*, you have the ingredients needed for a harmonious culmination of energy and matter, or what we call – life! She is our one and only true creator and most importantly, she is our nurture and true source of energy. Only through Mother Nature's splendor can life be created and can life forms evolve. Mother Nature intended humans to evolve into intelligent, civilized, human beings.

Why we cannot see this reality is due to the imaginary boundaries that we are taught to believe in. The earth and all of nature were created for man is a taught belief used to clog our minds and derail us from the truth! Today those imaginary boundaries have been lifted. This does not mean that God is dead; this means that God is alive in every-thing, especially in you, because mother nature is God, and you are mother nature! Through previous existences, the soul collects truths that only need to be awakened. My intentions were to unlock these hidden truths within each of you. For it is this genuine wisdom that is continuously repressed and pushes humans further away from the source that created them – mother nature.

Thomas Moore author of "CARE FOR THE SOUL" writes, "it's odd that religious leaders, so vocally concerned about sexual morality and faithfulness to a creed, have not been tireless in speaking on behalf of the earth and its creatures. Nature is the beginning of spiritual wisdom and the irreplaceable matrix of the soul." Much of humanity has grown cynical, we hide away in our churches praying and paying for spiritual guidance. We donate countless dollars to interpreters rendering their opinion of some books written for humans, millenniums ago. Sadly, these scriptures have done more damage than good, for both earth and humanity.

If we are nation under the God of Moses, then we permit ourselves to be a nation under the devil as well. To believe in one fallacy is to believe in the other. To believe in neither, is to successfully lift one of the most crucial and blinding imaginary boundaries of all time. If a large portion of humans believe that their way is the truth and another believes that theirs is the truth, then we can *never* see the truth, that we are <u>one</u>. Such is the case now for the Christian faith. You have Protestants, Lutherans, Baptists, Apologetics, Pentecost, Catholics, Evangelicals, Methodist, Orthodox, Jehovah's Witnesses, Mormons, just to name a few; all under one faith, yet they cannot even see themselves as one, because they are so blinded by their endless chase for an unauthentic God and their eagerness to be the one who represents the absolute truth.

However, if we can learn to become one with nature, in the way that Jesus did, then we will secure our future in such a way, that earth will become an everlasting kingdom and your soul will continue its universal path of vitality in its pursuit of happiness. Each life will be brighter and more creative than in the past. Each rebirth will be better and more extraordinary than the last.

That is why it is so important to make all of earth creative, safe, and beautiful, because each time we are reincarnated we will be born with the confidence that each of us will be free from control and torture and have the *right* to life, liberty, and the pursuit of happiness. We need to become that example for the rest of the world now.

Humans were brought into life by mother nature; It is she that is refining our minds and intelligence throughout our human evolutionary journey. We (the United States) shall become protectors of nature; a proud nation that saves forest and species and stands strong for equality in all humans. We had forgotten collectively where we come from, yet she's been here all along, allowing us to slowly awaken to the real truth.

From the book, "<u>ANYTHING WE LOVE CAN BE SAVED</u>" author Alice Walker writes common sense when she wrote, "It is fatal to love a God who does not love you. All people deserve to worship a God who also worships them. A God that made them and likes them, that is why nature, Mother Earth is such a good choice."

When we realize that nature is our true God, and that she loves us, we can begin to show the love and appreciation to Mother Nature that we do to the made-up God of Moses; our world will open up and the universe will pour it's harmonious blessings upon us, because we will be aligned with our true spirit.

History proves in abundance that one can live without religion, but no one has ever lived without Mother Nature. Not one person! Think about that for a moment and how honest and significant this statement is. All of the foods we eat, the fluids that keep us alive, the air that we breathe, it's all Mother Nature, she is our source of vitality.

Humans often think that we are a separate entity from nature or that we are superior to her, as if she was created for our sake; but in reality, we are a product of nature and we were created for her sake, to experience life, through the eyes of humanity.

We cannot see that we are one with nature, because religions and political societies teach us that nature was created for us and/or that there are no effects of global warming, or that the earth and nature are somehow evil. All of this misinformation is not only hurting nature, but humanity as well.

America's Motto is "In God we Trust" hence, through this God of Moses, we have become the most powerful country in the world. So powerful that we can kill everyone and everything that exists upon that face of the earth at any moment. A nation guided by those who protect nature would trust in nature.

Nature would not permit nations to act like animals, for nature intended humans to differ than the rest of the animal kingdom. To become a nation guided by nature and science is to see past all imaginary boundaries. Only then can we truly be the land of the free and only then can the world follow in our bravery and become one. From here on forward, you have a choice; you can follow the herd to the edge of the cliff and jump off or you can learn to follow your heart and begin the reconstruction of creativity and righteousness here on earth!

Sooner or later,
we will have to
recognize that the Earth
has rights, too,
to live without pollution.
What mankind must know
is that human beings
cannot live without
Mother Earth,
but the planet
can live without
humans.

Evo Moreles

- <u>Wasted Energy</u> -

In order to change the world for the better we must first change our thoughts. In America alone, millions abuse and/or are severely addicted to alcohol. Countless have died due to alcohol and/or alcohol related incidents all around the world. This flammable liquid has burned humanity since it's very existence and will continue to do so as long as it exists.

From the "POOR RICHARD'S ALMANIC", Benjamin Franklin offers some words of wisdom with this key phrase; "He that spills the rum loses that only, he that drinks it, often loses both that and himself." Teenagers all across America are finding themselves binge drinking on regular basis. The age requirements to purchase and consume alcohol is irrelevant, for over 70% of students say that they have drank alcohol prior to the age of 18, most by the tenth grade.

Each year, there are millions of spousal abuse cases reported, alcohol is almost often the fuel behind the fire. In prison, most individuals will attest to being under the influence of alcohol and other drugs, while committing their crimes. It is obvious that alcohol abuse has negative effects on humanity, for it impairs the human mind and can unleash the most negative, selfish thoughts and actions within people.

In the previous chapter, we mentioned that there is no evil in this world. However, there are people thinking negative thoughts and acting upon them. Every mind is powerful, for it can either build or destroy. Your precious mind is of no exception, you could think positive or negative, productive or destructive, but what you can't be is your true optimal self while overly intoxicated.

When alcohol consumption reaches high levels, the mind and the body can become dysfunctional. A person that over pollutes his or body with alcohol becomes unaware of their actions, so unaware, that he or she will fail to possess the most crucial sense of all, your common sense. Nevertheless, senseless acts will inevitably occur.

Many drunken individuals become egotistical, aggressive, and destructive to the point where they will do harm to themselves and/or anyone around them. Sadly, they often do the most harm to those who love them the most, like family and friends. We have declared this war on drugs, when America's <u>legal</u> drugs have been killing more than the drugs, we are war with.

One thing that has remained consistent over the last 40 years is that close to half a million people die each year from tobacco related incidents alone. Once again, the required age to purchase tobacco is oblivious because nearly 90% of all smokers began smoking before the age of 18. Everyone in America remains blind and allows this ignorance to continue. It's clear that tobacco and alcohol kill, and can lead to endless suffering and damages, just as <u>legal</u> firearms do. Why do we tolerate this? Because these "legal" entities bring in hundreds of billions of dollars in revenue to our government.

The Declaration of Independence clearly states that it is our duty to gain control over a government that has become destructive of life, liberty, and the pursuit of happiness. If you could see beyond imaginary boundaries, you will bear witness to a highly destructive government. Especially, the far right in congress who do nothing to even bring these topics to light, instead they spend their time and energy trying to impeach everyone on the left, or harassing rainbows, and victims of mass shootings.

Every year blinded individuals are lured into spending hundreds of billions of dollars on a cause that is just suicidal and unworthy. They are aware of this yet will do nothing to prevent these legal entities that are truly harming us, except for the occasional label warning. Why? The reason is obvious; our government's love for money overpowers their love for life and humanity. For example, the NRA donates hundreds of millions of dollars each year to our right-wing politicians, so that they do not enforce stricter laws.

Alcohol is a negative altering mind stimulant; overindulgence in alcohol can lead to a hangover or even death. Overindulgence in alcohol, as fun as it may seem to some, produces negative results, not just in thought, but also in body. Those that feel there is no negative impact towards being addicted to alcohol are those that will suffer the most from it in their latter days.

Alcohol has caused millions of marriages to end and millions of ordinary people to beat, mistreat, cheat and/or sexually abuse their loved ones. Far too many are ruined financially, spiritually, and emotionally.

Today we see many people who have veered off into the deep end, begging for change and living on the streets. People blinded by imaginary boundaries call them bums and write them off, yet they are human beings, no different than you and me. They are our brothers and sisters. Every city in the United States has its share of homeless individuals; however, few humans will uplift or truly extend a helping hand. We simply neglect them or donate petty change hoping to never see them again, as does our government.

A portion of the Governments collected wealth that is accumulated by the people should be used to improve life for the people. Humans working to help other humans is what will make this world a better place. America needs not to meddle in foreign affairs nor lands, but instead improve the quality of life here on our land for our people. The US Military should become a force working together to help our country. One force striving to improve this country can set examples to the other countries of the world.

No longer should we train our youth to kill; instead, we must train them, to help us with our communities, to heal. We must work together to revitalize neighborhoods that have been neglected and/or that have suffered from natural disasters. When catastrophes occur, our United Forces should be here and readily available to assist. These storms are intensifying as humanity continues to destroy and pollute mother nature and we need to be prepared.

The world and its inhabitants have suffered enough and now it is time to open our eyes and dismiss certain opinions that have become laws. Like the sinister command to kill. No one has the right to kill or order someone to be killed. The right to kill should be taken away in all of its forms for every human being and/or political agenda.

Mother nature decides who lives or dies, not man. We must learn not to cause, allow, or applaud any unnatural deaths. Therefore, we must ban the death penalty in all its forms because it is not anyone's "God Given Right" to decide who lives or dies. When we as species, allow our government to kill humans for whatever reason, we are not allowing the soul of these individuals to regret, nor learn from their mistake and thus, countless of criminals are carrying within themselves past life regressions. Understand this, if we do not teach these individuals, the lessons of his or her crime, in this lifetime, then this energy will be reborn into the same pattern, in the subsequent life. Such individuals cannot be put to death or simply rot in prison but must educate themselves and learn why he or she committed these crimes, or these crimes will be embedded in their soul and acted out in a future lifetime.

My great, great, uncle was one of the first men to be put to death in Texas for boot-legging alcohol. He died in vain, because his death was based on creating an illegal substance that has now made its way into mainstream America. My point is not to push for alcohol to become illegal; instead, my intentions were to point out, that we mustn't sentence anyone to death, under any circumstances, whatsoever. How can someone want to take away women's rights and claim to be pro-life yet, enforce the death penalty? We're taking away the wrong freedoms from the wrong people.

The opinion that has become a law to bear firearms must be restricted to all humans. Not everything that is written in the bible is correct and certainly not everything that is written in the US constitution is correct as well. We have abolished slavery because it was wrong, now we must abolish the right to bear arms, or it will continue to be the number one killer of our children and teens in the US and the primary reason we have so many mass shootings in this country.

Mother nature does not condone, favor, or recognize costumes. Hence, no person alive should have the right to take another person's life. The minute you come out of the womb is when you are born, when you take that first breath, you are born, and every person born should have the right to life, liberty, and the pursuit happiness. We should also have peace of mind, knowing that we are safe in our communities; in short, there can never be peace and heaven on earth with firearms everywhere.

In the simplest manner, firearms must be banned for everyone in America, especially in our cities. This includes all those who serve as law enforcement and those associated with the government. In 2022, there were 64 police officers murdered in the line of duty. In that same year, law enforcement officers shot and killed 1,192 civilians. This should be unacceptable and upsetting to you, that we are caught up in a society that is so full of fear that they feel that they need guns. All because gun manufacturers want to profit and simply do not value life! This also shows that "Good Guys" with guns is not the solution, because many of those "Good Guys" have lost their common sese!

There is a solution that will take some effort and mainly some common sense, but more than anything; we the people will have to make a choice. It will require that enough of us are fed up with our government and their inability to make real gun law changes. Changes that will hurt their feeling, as mentioned before, by revoking their second amendment rights, but it will save countless lives.

I will point out the real solution here in the following paragraphs, but you on the right will do nothing with this knowledge, because you are blinded by your greed and are slaves to these gun manufacturers, that donate to you in exchange for your silence. Nevertheless, here is the <u>real</u> solution to lowering gun violence in America.

In places like Tokyo, Japan, where there are no firearms allowed, and policemen are highly trained in martial arts, (meaning they do not carry firearms) you'll find one of the safest cities on earth, for they are essentially connected within, meaning they do not need cowardly weapons. We must take note of the success of other countries, we must shut down firearms manufacturers and all those who sell, trade or raffle firearms in America. Equip our officers with inner-confidence and courage; not fear and firearms.

Japan as a country, has one of the lowest gun-related death rates in the world. Why? Here is the solution, from businessinsider.com, "Japan which has strict laws for obtaining firearms, seldom has more than 10 shooting deaths a year in a population of 127 million people. If Japanese people want to own a gun, they must attend an all-day class, pass a written test, and achieve at least 95% accuracy during a shooting range test. Then they have to pass a mental-health evaluation at a hospital, as well as a background check, in which the government digs into any criminal records or ties and interviews friends and family members. Finally, they can buy only shotguns and air rifles – no handguns – and must retake the class and the initial exam every three years." That's why!

This is common sense gun control proven to work and that is how we get control of our overwhelming problem. I would even like to add that if you are in the city; all guns must be banned, because most gun homicides happen in the inner city. Please take a close look at this chart below from our friends over at Everytown for gun safety, who genuinely care for human life. What stands out to you? What are we going to do about to resolve this issue?

The US gun homicide rate is 26 times that of other high-income countries.

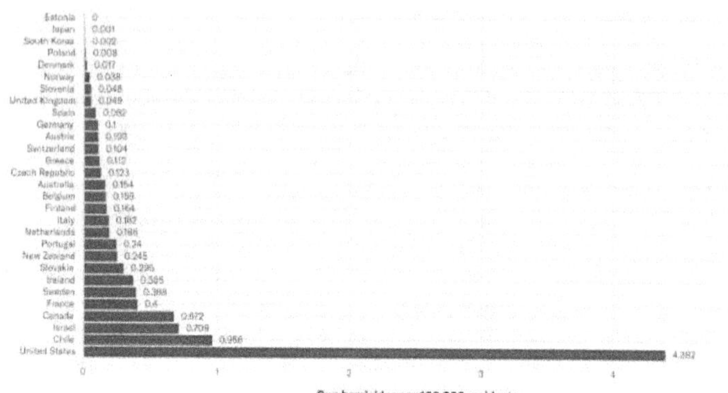

The place that I come from has a governor that is in complete opposition of what Japan is doing in order to keep its citizens safe. Here in the great state of Texas, there are virtually no rules, anyone can purchase firearms from gun shows, guns shops, shopping centers with sporting good departments, pawn shops, etc. In our state you cannot purchase alcohol until you are 21, yet you can purchase AR 15's at the age of 18 with absolutely none of the criteria that Japan request of their gun owners, none!

The city of Uvalde, Texas was tragically hit by this gruesome reality, yet no one blamed the governor for passing a law that allowed this to unfold. He acted stunned and dared to ask what we could do to prevent this from happening. There was innocent little children's blood all over his hands, yet not one person (for the exception of Beto

O'Rourke) stood up for them and said to the governor, this is your fault. Instead, we blamed everyone else; the time the law took to isolate the issue, the commanding officers, the schools inability to keep its doors locked, not having enough mental health facilities; but what about the idiot who granted permission for an 18-year-old to purchase multiple firearms (AR-15's) and an abundance of ammo legally just days apart without any background checks and for passing a permit less carry bill.

It utterly disgusts me how naive we as a species can be, by voting these ignorant states of mind into power. If more guns and looser laws were the solution, we would be one of the safest nations, but we are not, and it is time to wake up!

Here are some statics that I want you to soak in. We must see the harm that we are in, if we are to one day get out of it. These are not my opinions but actual statistics from the CDC. In the year 2021, 48,830 humans died from gun related injuries in America alone. More than half of those were suicides. Each year more than 140,000 people die from alcohol related incidents. There are more than 480,000 deaths every year from tobacco related incidents, that's more than alcohol, car accidents, Aids, murders and suicided combined. It's heartbreaking because each of these lives is someone's child, sibling, spouse, parent or loved one; moreover, each one of these deaths could have been prevented.

We must gain control over ourselves, as a whole. We must do this by educating humans on the dangers of America's cash crops, such as firearms, tobacco, and over-indulgence in alcohol. I am not talking about those who are sophisticated and drink sociably. Instead, it is those who need to drink in order to function. Those that get behind the wheel intoxicated and cause endless pain for families all around the world. Those who are so disconnected from nature and common sense that this life means nothing to them.

It is those people we must help so that we can live in a safer environment. We must educate our youth of the dangers of man-made drugs, like crystal meth, cocaine, heroin, and fentanyl, but we need to be honest and inform them that alcohol, nicotine, and prescribed drugs are just as dangerous if not more dangerous and are legal. It is these man-made drugs that disconnect people from each other from reality, from nature, and above all, from love.

- <u>One World Order</u> -

Many religious leaders are entwined with politics and feel that a government cannot run successful unless led by individuals who are led by the laws of God. Pat Robertson is an evangelical Christian that many of the mega churches today follow suit in his views and beliefs "There will never be world piece until God's people are given their rightful place of leadership at the top of the world. How can there be peace when drunkards, drug dealers, communist, atheist, New Age worshippers of Satan; secular humanist, oppressive dictators, and homosexuals are on top?"

Religious Leaders have always yearned to be correct and superior to all, this is why they must constantly reassure you that there is a God. They are not certain themselves, and they know that you are not certain either, however you are a profit of God and that is where their over enthusiasm comes from.

These mega churches are heavily influenced with Maga movement, to the point where some believe Trump is Moses or the second coming of Jesus. They believe in this new world order, or in today's world, it has evolved into Project 25 and is dedicated to bringing white evangelicals to run our government, and they have selected Trump to lead the way. If implemented it would basically give the Republican President the authority to overturn any laws that this deranged group does not see fit, meaning dictatorship. It proposes prejudice bills like all Trans people be put in jail. What they don't understand is when you are on wrong side of justice; it cannot prevail; because common sense and dignity overpower prejudice and hate, time and time again.

Take for example, there once lived a prophet named Mohammed, who invited the Jews and Christians to join him in a single faith and worship the same God of Moses. It is said that if both faith's (God's people) would have joined forces, they would have conquered the world. The moral of this story is that all religions vary, meaning God's people cannot see all as one. Each has a belief system that is interpreted as they see it and they have no intention of converting into the belief of another or even co-existing in agreement with others. The sad truth is world peace will <u>never</u> come from God's people, for God's people cannot see that we are all one. They will remain divided by their desire to overrule and overpower one another through unauthentic power. Draining each other of our energy and not connecting with the real source is unauthentic power.

These pastors blind the herds into believing that their way is the only way, not seeing the division that they are causing. These mega churches are tens of thousands of people who are receiving instruction on who to vote for, what to think and most crucially how to unconsciously discriminate and hate on others!

They are raking in millions of dollars of tax-free money, with their jets, expensive cars, and their lavish mansions. However, for their organizations to remain tax exempt under IRC Section 501(c)(3), religious leaders can't make partisan comments in official organization publications or at official church functions, meaning they cannot preach their opinion. Strange because almost all of them can be found on YouTube videos, voicing who to vote for and still none pays taxes and/or is ever fined. Why?

They want us to vote for a person who is, quite frankly, the most unreligious candidate to ever run for any position in government and who has caused the most damage to our country with his big lies and bogus claims! I often hear the religious right saying, "he's my president and he can do no wrong." Well, he sure has fooled all of us, for like Moses, he fed us lies and half of us believed it to be truth. How can we compare the life of Jesus who came down to serve and not judge, to a complete moron that has been accused of rape, sexual assault, and sexual harassment to at least twenty-five different women? He's spews racism and hatred and has been indicted for a legion of felony crimes.

The hate he breeds is the most harmful prominent issue that we face in America today. It has awoken the most negatives of negatives that we were once on track to overcoming as a nation; namely, racism, extreme evangelical authoritarian and the oppression of human rights.

Everything the extreme right brings forth is critical and destructive to humanity. Take for example; homosexuality can be found in various species throughout the world. Nature has endowed plenty, the love or desire for same sex relationships. These are the laws of nature. It is her way of controlling the population of a species, yet religious and political fanatics cannot see this reality. Human beings are no exception to the laws of nature, yet people blinded by these imaginary boundaries consider these fellow humans as evil.

Religion treats these individuals with such disgrace and acts as if they are inhumane and this why. In Romans 1:27 Paul Writes, "And likewise also the men, leaving the natural use of the women, burned in their lust toward another: men with men working that which is unseemly… unrighteousness, maliciousness; full of envy, murder, debate, deceit, malignity; whispers, back biters, haters of God, despiteful, proud, boasters, inventors of evil things, disobedient to parents, without under-standing, covenant breakers, without natural affections, implacable, unmerciful."

It is a well-known fact that one who cuts others down is attempting to lift himself up. Paul's opinion of homosexuality is given with such discrimination and hatred. In order to label any human in this manner is to be insecure about yourself. Throughout history, bible believers have treated homosexuals as if "the devil" has control over them. These individuals have been victims of a hate wave that has mentally and physically oppressed their life, liberty, and their pursuit of happiness. Today, in every single, race, culture, and nation you will find that homosexuality and trans people are present.

Most people in America, with the exception of the religious right and other hate groups like them, have come to accept that these individuals are not wicked as Paul describes, but merely humans. They have broken through a long struggle of imaginary boundaries brought on by people blinded by religion. Like the slaves and women, LGTB+ community is working its way out of the grips of religious suppression and beginning to live free, as nature intended them to be. Unfortunately, the intolerance written within the holy bible has made life a living hell for so many individuals throughout history.

While a fictional God has been wrongfully praised and offers a description of how we must live in order to enter his fantasy kingdom; humanities true creator, mother nature, is spreading a different kind of message, save your kingdom and be only your true self. There are millions of same sex relationships, and it is time that they be treated equally, just as opposite sex relationships are treated equally.

We are in no position to judge anyone person, but ourselves. Who a person lies with is no business to me, nor should it be to you, as long as it is consensual and as long as it is legal. When you judge humans from the LGTB+ community, you are saying to the creator that what she created is not sufficient to your liking. You are assuming that the creator made a mistake. Even from a Christian standpoint, you are saying God, I am above you now and I will be the one who will judge these people today because you made a mistake in creating them this way.

Homosexuals are born homosexual; they are not tempted or talked into being gay. Trying to convert them is like asking a straight person to be gay when they are straight. Think about that for a minute. I know some will say, "God saved me," but those people who have been "saved" are either lying to themselves or were not born gay. They were born bisexual, and there is significant difference.

Understand now that Mother Nature created you just the way she intended to. Each life that we are reincarnated into, we are born into a new body, this body may not be the gender you were in the previous life (male or female) but your love for that gender may have stayed the same, it's ok; mother nature made you this way and accepts you as you are. No one has the right to judge anyone, for any reason whatsoever; especially because of few authors voiced their wicked opinions in a book millenniums ago.

When we can start to live by this code, the code of decency, life will be as it was intended to be, beautiful and prosperous with love. You will be the light that you were meant to be, and you will not be corrupted or darkened by others.

To control or judge anyone is to lack self-control and self-confidence. All a human owns is their mind and the thoughts that enter it; gain control of this and you will never need to control, abuse, judge or build yourself up by means of tearing others down again. As Plato once said, "To conquer thy self is the greatest accomplishment of all" to conquer yourself is to never feel insecure of others, regardless of how indifferent they may appear to you.

While political and religious leaders struggle for power in their battles for global dominance, it is extremely important to remember that they work for you. You feed them, you lead them, not vice versa. Since their existence, imaginary bound derived societies have controlled and blinded the masses, rather than the people controlling them. Since money is what funds individuals of these societies, it is money we must control. We live in a political system that has transmitted, with taxpayers' money, the most horrendous inventions of all time, and yet our leaders (worldwide) are crying for more money to enhance warfare technology, making warfare our top priority on earth.

We the people must unite to become the commonsense authority that holds these people accountable for their devastating ways. By neglecting our duties, comes even greater kings of terror and future lifetimes of suffering. There is no such thing as something for nothing, and that something that we will receive is – Power.

The power to decide what our money will be spent on moving forward and the power to review what our money has been spent on. We must inherit the power to deal with it and/or delete it according to its nature. All thoughts or ideas that have surpassed the true review of the awakening people, by being previously produced shall be decided as either productive or destructive, then dealt with in a commonsense manner.

Anything that is unbeneficial to humanity and nature must be terminated without further manufacturing. Any law that has counteracted nature and her established laws should no longer co-exist.

No longer should any company have the right to pollute our water, land, and air, no matter how much they pay our government. Nor should we allow these political leaders and corporate giants to tear down the remaining forest that they have left us with, leading to the ruination of hundreds of thousands of species, the ozone layer and eventually all things, through global warming. We cannot go backwards in our transition of turning green and finding other ways to create energy without polluting the earth, like Project 25 intends us to.

The issue is that the religious right does not believe in global warming, so it is our responsibility to save us and them, because they are too blind and dimwitted to see the reality of our negative effects. Why? Because everything about their views is about "I" and not – We!

We should NOT allow the continuation of weapon manufacturing; as it is now, there are rarely any woods to hunt in, much less, any real hunters. If you live way out in the country and we follow suit with Japan's strict gun laws, then I say that is perfectly fine to own a single shot rifle or shotgun. But let's be ultimately realistic here, all other guns must immediately come to a halt in production. I don't care how much they donate to the right wing; human life is priceless, and too much blood has been shed in the name of silence. It is time to speak up and make it illegal to carry firearms anywhere in the city and moreover to produce and sell them in America.

A real hunter does not include handguns or AR 15 in his attack; only foolish punks, full of fear hunt their prey in such a spiritless manner. That stands true on the streets and in the jungle; only a real coward uses firearms. America needs not to focus on the other countries of the world for now; instead, America must learn to focus within.

Understand this, so-called leaders, and evangelicals of the world; until people who are *not* blinded by imaginary boundaries are leading the way, this country, and this world for that matter, will never be at peace or be safe. Proof of this, is the top countries where they are not blinded by religion, such places like Denmark, Japan, Sweden, and Norway just to a name a few have some of the lowest crime rates and also the lowest gun violence in the world. It is because they see things differently.

Un-blind yourselves now and abolish from your mind and soul, the negativity that is erasing out humanity. It is called intolerance and ignorance, but you have been armed with the proper energy to defeat it – it's called your common sense!

You did not come this far in this book to turn away and do nothing, once your soul acknowledges the universal truths written within these pages, you cannot go backwards. Once a child knows that Santa Clause isn't real, as sad as it may be, they cannot be fooled into re-believing in him. He or she can grow up and be Santa-like, but they cannot go backwards. The same is true for adults, once you know deep within your soul, these universal truths that I have revealed throughout this book are true, and you cannot go backwards into believing the fallacies of life!

What can you do to
promote world peace?
Go home and
love your family.

Mother Teresa

(68)

-**Kingdom Come**-

It has been predicted since words could be formulated that earth will end. This way of thinking has led us to the means in which the world can end, not naturally, but instead through human causes. If we are to change the world for the better, we must first change our thoughts and become aware of our consciousness and actions.

We have exposed many of the negative thoughts, opinions and beliefs that have plagued humanity. Opposite of destructive or negative energy is positive energy. Humans can destroy creations and take life, or they can build them up and breathe into them purpose. Man can commit horrific acts of terrorism, or he can produce works of wonder. Humans can be either positive or negative at any time through their emotions and thoughts.

Through the aid of creative imagination, humans have transited portions of earth into places of pure excitement and joy. To display this tremendous power of creative imagination; look no further than the spectacular worlds of Disney. Here, people of all ethnicities, cultures, countries and religious societies are brought together by the power of creative imagination and thought. Here humans are joined in peace to view and enjoy the creativity we each possess inside.

Every poverty-stricken land is the result of lack of creative imagination and lack of faith and overall, negligence. We, meaning all humans, must work together to use our creative imagination in such a way that we transform all parts of the world into creative states of being. Humans do not abuse alcohol, kill one another, destroy nature, or attempt to convert any belief into another at the wonderful theme parks of Walt Disney. All the labels people give themselves are dissolved here; here humans are just humans, brought together as one to experience the magic of creative imagination. A magic that we each possess within.

When our world is refined with such creativity and amazement, violence and ignorance will begin to perish. I am not suggesting that every street becomes a Disney Park, what I am proposing is that we use are resources to make every street refined, productive and safe.

It will cost money to rebuild such a wonderful world, and the right will defy it all the way, (because that is what they do) yet the money used will go to saving lives, rather than destroying life, as is the case now, for warfare technology. The inner cities of North America are in need of such transitions, because the more creative and resourceful a city becomes the less destruction and violent it will be. We have to bring light to darkness if we are to succeed in making America a better place. When we accomplish this, other countries will follow suite and our world will transform for the better.

The people of these communities should assist in such revitalizations, so that they will experience the positive feeling of achievement. The more we shift our universal conscious to creative and positive states of mind and living, the more joyous and fulfilled our lives will become. Remember, every life that we are undoubtedly born into will be better, more prosperous, and more meaningful this way.

We will learn to celebrate and take pride in all of our accomplishments and creative endeavors, moreover we will celebrate our cultures and traditions, rather than fight and kill over them. Humans do not realize the ultimate power our minds possess, much less how to fully harness this power.

> I believe this, frightfulness we
> see everywhere today is only
> temporary. Tomorrow will be
> better for as long as America keeps
> alive the ideals of freedom and a better life.
>
> Walt Disney

-<u>The Subconscious Mind</u>-

As you are reading, you are feeding your subconscious mind. The subconscious mind can translate both negative and positive thought impulses into reality. The subconscious mind works continuously throughout life, whether one makes any effort to influence it or not, it even works when we are asleep. Dreams can take us deep into infinite intelligence, where our soul can connect and recharge with the intangible energy we derive from.

In your dreams, you may find yourself surprisingly familiar with certain unknown places or people, even though you may have never been to these places or met these people, your soul has. This is possible through the portion of the brain known as the subconscious mind. This is why many wise minds say; to sleep is to be alive, but to awaken is to die; this is because the soul is infinite, and the subconscious mind is unlimited.

Many question where dreams and/or ideas come from, such individuals are not fully aware of the subconscious mind and how it functions. In short, the subconscious mind is like a sponge, absorbing everything, when squeezed it releases the liquids it has absorbed. Likewise depending upon what you feed the subconscious mind or don't, determines to all the kind of knowledge you educate yourself with. The subconscious mind will absorb, and then translate into reality that which has been absorbed. If the majority a person absorbs in life is of a negative nature, then by the laws of nature, this person is more liable to think and act upon their negative impulses of desire.

Humans have the power to control their dominating thoughts and more importantly they have the power to influence their subconscious mind. With this knowledge, all humans are capable of controlling their earthly destiny and overall, the earth's destiny. People who believe themselves doomed to failure or poverty are creators of their own misfortunes, just as people who believe and think themselves into success and riches.

What you choose to feed the subconscious mind is a direct result of who you are and what your circumstances will be. If you fail to feed or influence the subconscious mind, it will translate into reality, the thoughts that reach it as a result of your neglect. So, it is very important to understand this power of mind.

The subconscious mind is also an intermediate for transition, it's a mental converter. When one prays to *any* chosen God, he or she is in reality praying to their subconscious mind. The subconscious mind will pick up on those thoughts, prayers or desires that are backed by faith and prepare them for transition.

We do this every single day and the most basic example that I can provide you with is, when we are thinking of what to eat; we begin to desire this particular food, perhaps from this particular place, we can virtually taste it and begin desiring it strongly. Eventually we eat that particular meal.

I want you to take a trip into your imagination and I want for you to recall some of your strongest desires and thoughts that have become reality. Such as your spouse or partner, your children, your business endeavors, or your material possessions, such as money, cars, and houses. You must realize that before you received any of these entities, you first desired them and your subconscious mind has brought them into your reality.

Desire is the starting point to all achievement and the subconscious mind is what wheels us into attaining those desires. In the same manner that Mother Nature drafted us into being, your subconscious mind transits our intangible impulses of energy into reality.

When one prays to any God and/or any deity that they believe in, the subconscious mind is picking up on the impulses of extreme desire and preparing them for whatever means of transition. Whether those thoughts are positive, or negative is irrelevant to the subconscious mind, for all it detects is the fire in your desire.

As he or she prays for the things most desired, then suddenly receives that which has been concentrated upon, his or her belief in that God excels. What really occurs is through the portion of the mind known as creative imagination, one comes into direct communication with infinite intelligence, and then, if it detects strong faith or you think about it obsessively, the sub-conscious mind will kick in and begin transitioning that into reality. Which is why I say it doesn't matter who you pray to, all that matters is how much faith you have, the subconscious mind will do the rest!

Infinite intelligence is the universal mind that drafted us into being. Anyone can tap into infinite intelligence, but only through the use of creative imagination through entities like brainstorming, meditation, prayer, and sleep. Those who use their intuition are those fortunate enough to connect with infinite intelligence. Everyone has within them all the true answers to all of life's most meaningful questions.

Everything that has ever been thought, every configuration on earth that has been produced or designed and everything we now know or will soon acknowledge, is readily available through creative imagination for anyone to receive.

Humans who create, invent or engineer, simply acknowledge and transmit the intangible from the endless storehouse of infinite intelligence. It is this phenomenal power of mind combined with courage, that has led humans to fulfill their inner most desires, such as flying in the sky, landing on the moon or wherever humans shall voyage to next in this universe, will only be possible through the power of creative imagination, faith, and the subconscious mind.

When we understand how these parts of our brain operate, we can begin to influence and control our own circumstances, meaning we can truly co-create whatever we want with Mother Nature and truly create heaven on earth. Even one of the greatest minds of all time stated that, "Imagination is more important than knowledge." It was Einstein's imagination that made him a genius, but you have this tremendous power within you too, perhaps waiting to be unleashed.

When one is connected to purpose through creative imagination, your soul will feel so aligned with the universe. This happens for example when a singer/song writer is in a studio recording their song. If that is their soul's purpose, the connection they feel with the universe is harmonious because they are connected to spirit in that moment, and there is no greater moment than that. When we are in our purpose, we are one with the universe and anything is possible!

Logic will get you from A to B.
Imagination will take you everywhere!

Albert Einstein

(73)

- **Human Emotions** -

When impulses or intentions of thought are blended with emotions, actions inevitably occur. Emotions are intangible forms of energy; yet these energies have the power to influence your thoughts and dictate your actions. Many humans go through life <u>unable</u> or unaware of how to control their emotions and so it is necessary to absorb and learn the following information. When we have all of these individuals that murder, rape, molest, abuse, and/or any other offenses similar to these crimes blame this and that for their ignorant actions, it is their actions that speak louder than words and express the true inner intentions.

Our country is divided right now more than ever because of misleading information, conspiracy theories and lies. I know that sex trafficking exists, and it is terrible thing, however it has always existed. Please understand that sexual assault crimes and sex trafficking of minors pre-dates even the bible. However, scriptures from the Old Testament are full of instructions "from God" ordering to take young women virgins and do what they please with them. Today these instructions are still followed and there is not one brand of Christianity (or religion) that can cast a stone to another, because <u>ALL</u> religious establishments have child sexual abuse tied to them.

Some of the most trusted institutions that we entrust with our children are actually some of the biggest pedophiles of this world, like the boy scouts of America and many of our church leaders. Those blinded by conspiracy theories do not need to make up delusions of celebrities and left-wing politicians, who they assume are sex traffickers and drinking the blood of our children, when we have real pedophiles all around us.

This is the energy that is dividing us, because half of us can see reality, while the other half cannot think for themselves. Ironically, many of these leaders that are condemning people to "hell" are often those who do the most immoral acts to our children and to humanity. If they start off in this world being tortured by the ones that they are supposed to trust in, then we have failed to do our job and protect our youth as a society. Conspiracy theories derail us from solving the real issues we face, like the number one killer of kids and teens in America - Gun Violence! If you really care about our youth, and you say you are Pro Life, then go to battle for them, because this is where they really need our help more than ever; to make gun laws that will save them.

-<u>The Success Cycle</u>-

Your soul is your energy, no soul, no life. When a soul gives life to the tangible patterns of matter that align with its desired characteristics and persona, the soul has chosen its destiny. Everyone is here for a purpose and though the aid of creative imagination, you can find yours. Numerous professions have unfolded, giving humans an array of career opportunities to strive for, but some are not yet discovered.

Today the development of professions continues to broaden. In comparison to millennium ago or even a half century ago, most individuals are now faced with so many choices, that it becomes like trying to find a needle in the haystack. There are many humans that will search an entire lifetime trying to find their calling. Others will completely ignore searching for their purpose and will be herded to the *comfort zone*.

Understand now that those who succeed in all walks of life are not those who work the hardest, nor those who quit, but instead those that choose to think and work smarter. Just like a metal detector can detect a needle in a haystack, your soul is also a detector capable of attracting one's true calling. When your soul acknowledges its purpose the energy within you will surge, alerting you to your true calling. For many, the desire to succeed alone will spark new career opportunities, even if it does not exist. When more people are on their righteous path, the safer and more creative this world can be.

If success is what you seek then look no further, for all true success's will begin within. Success is always manifested from an idea, thought, vision or dream, backed by strong desire. We each possess the ability to turn our desires into reality, through the sub-conscious mind; however, most of us do not know how to harness this power, because we are not taught this in school. Since we each perceive the world differently, we each desire various forms of success.

There is one desire that links all of the universe's energies together and that is the desire to exist. The desire to exist is the strongest of all desires, it is the reason that we are here now in this stage of evolution. Human desires consist of the desire to find true love, one's true calling, wealth, good health, freedom, power, fame, peace and spiritual enrichment.

One formula, which enables humans in all callings, to succeed and long enjoy their success is exemplified in the following. This formula has been used since the first humans tuned into their imagination and unleashed their inner most desires. If you repeat to your subconscious mind, the following techniques about to be revealed, you will unlock the possibility of receiving all that you truly desire from life. Desire is as you know that starting point to all successes and/or achievements. If there is no desire, then there is no sense in success. Desires vary and/or differ for everyone. Humans have transformed countless desires into their physical equivalency.

Here is a common desire that many humans struggle with, the desire to lose weight. How can we successfully lose weight if most of us do not even know how to succeed? How can we succeed in saving this planet from self-destruction if we cannot even save ourselves? It is said that American dieters spend well over 70 billion dollars a year trying to gain control over unwanted weight, yet 95% of diets fail. That is a lot of money that we as a country are spending on failing. Almost 70% of Americans are overweight or classify as obese.

This excess body mass leads people to many health issues, such as diabetes, high blood pressure, heart disease, and certain cancers. Of course, there are many means by which one can shed the pounds off. The problem lies in the teachings that food intake must be limited to insignificant portions. This is avoiding the laws of nature, for matter must consume matter, if it is to survive. We cannot live off of just water. Humans, just like any other species that nature has created is intended to continuously eat as a primary source of energy.

If you do not eat, the body will begin to eat itself. If you neglect this law of nature, your body will begin to feed off of its own muscle. This may appear as weight loss; however, this weight loss method is unhealthy and unsuccessful in true body fitness. Understand that there is neither diet, nor doctor that can shape you into a miracle, because the miracle must come from within.

The first principle to success is you cannot cheat yourself to success, avoid short cuts at all cost. If you desire to lose weight, get in shape, or attain success in any other field, you must prepare yourself mentally and envision yourself as you wish to be beforehand. You have to see yourself as if you have already lost weight, so the subconscious mind can begin to translate that into reality. If you cannot vision yourself losing weight, or believe that you cannot lose weight, then you are right, as Mr. Henry Ford would say, "Whether you think you can, or you think you can't – you're right." This stands true for everything you do in life. It all starts in your mind, once you can conceive it, you must believe in it, only then can you achieve it!

The second principle is you must put in the work, meaning you must physically exercise as a habit and eat right. It is so easy and convenient nowadays to eat fast food. When you are young you can get away with it for some time, but eventually it will catch up to you, because we are not meant to eat this way every day. We are not designed by nature to process all these trans-fat, saturated fats, processed foods, and intake these high in sugar, salt, calorie items. These are the foods that cause cancer within us.

Hundreds of Millions of people have died before their time, simply by avoiding regular exercise of the mind, body, and spirit. Although it is not written clearly in history, human beings must continuously feed the mind, body, and spirit, but they must also exercise them or they will become weak, allowing others to prey upon them. We must learn to become one with nature; she can nurture us into optimal healthy human beings and protect us from the negative elements that come with failure.

Overweight humans are aware of their disorder and should not be around those of a negative or destructive mind, as is the case for attaining all successes. We must surround ourselves with positive affirmations and positive alliances if we are to succeed in any endeavor. These people need more than anything the influence of love, hope, and faith. They need determination and support of those who are aligned; mind, body, and soul with them throughout their recovery.

It is essential that we realize they may need our support not our judgement; for these individuals live in fear, the fear of criticism, the fear of ill health and the fear of death. If fear is detected by the subconscious mind all physical and productive action is eliminated. Driven by emotions of fear, many overweight individuals are unable to successfully accomplish their desired weight loss, and, in such cases, this fear can destroy other desires, including the most significant desire of all, the desire to exist.

The opposite of success is failure, the only known cure for failure – is faith! Understand that the *faith* in your desires will determine the outcome or resolution of your success. You can pray or manifest anything you want to achieve, but you have to have faith and believe in it. The humans who have engaged faith in their desires are those who have succeeded in all walks of life.

The mind that believes it will win and triumph is the mindset that will always win. You cannot just be confident; you have to be convinced. Through faith, various individuals and/or groups have amazed the world by creating what appears to be miracles, all so-called miracles are nothing more or less than acts of faith.

For thousands of years, humanity has mistakenly linked faith as product connected only to the religious society. When in fact, faith has nothing to do with religion, for it is a state of mind, states of minds are human choices and when one chooses to induce thoughts backed by faith to the subconscious mind, it will translate those thoughts into reality.

It is extremely important to recognize and apply faith to all which you desire, if you fail to follow this simple procedure, be prepared to meet failure. Understand that to successfully lose weight or attain any other goal in life for that matter, we must have faith in ourselves and faith in what you believe in. As I mentioned before, the subconscious mind will translate anything you want, as long as you have faith in it.

Before the existence of any God, humans were bringing into reality what they could imagine and believe. Faith was at work, thousands of years prior to the conception of any dogma, creed, or religion; in fact, through faith and creativity, all of these things emerged. The scriptures of the bible are not inspired by God; they are inspired by the subconscious minds of the authors who retained knowledge of stories and teachings inspired by ancient civilizations, like the Egyptians, the Greeks, and the Romans.

Although they are presented as original, many stories from the scriptures were like the stories of that time, retold and adapted, just with different characters, cultures, locations, and times. The author's subconscious minds were like sponges absorbing all the information of their time and then modifying these stories as the ultimate truth.

(78)

Faith is not owned by any one religion. Study history and will see that this is true. From Moses's creation story to the resurrection story, to Jesus walking on water; all of these stories were told in different cultures prior to them making into the bibles. I'm not saying that everything in the bible is untrue; there are many moral teachings and well intentions in it, but the same is true for all religions across the world. Our morality does not come from the scriptures or any one religion, but rather from our common sense.

If a person from Asia prays to Buddha, or a human from India prays to Krishna, or a Jew to the God of Hebrews, or an atheist who may not pray to a deity or even an astrologer to the stars; it's ok, as long as they have faith in what they believe in, then they can attain any success they desire. Meaning any God or lack of one can deliver results, because the real God is built in you, it's your subconscious mind connecting with the universal mind, backed by faith!

Have faith in yourself and faith in Nature. Faith is the antidote to failure and nature's cure for all illnesses. Through faith the human species emerged and can survive and continue to evolve well beyond the path we are currently headed. Faith is the solid foundation of all who have succeeded and all who will succeed in any undertaking. Faith is within you; harness it, treasure it, become it because you were born from it. Have good faith in everything you do, and you can never go wrong.

Believe in yourself.
Have Faith in your abilities.
Without a humble but reasonable
confidence in your own powers
you cannot be successful or happy.

Norman Vincent Peale

-<u>Negative Success</u>-

Not one society that has originated from the imaginary boundaries of our mind strives to teach humans the formula of success. Everyone has a choice to succeed or fail based upon his or her dominating thoughts. Whatever you think, you shall become, for these are laws of nature and they cannot be deviated. A mind can succeed for good or for all the wrong reasons. People thinking negative thoughts will have negative outcomes, meaning negative thoughts produce negative actions. I want you to understand the difference.

Negative success is usually a quick form of success, followed by a negative or destructive reaction, such as unnatural death, self-destruction through legal and/or illegal drugs, suicide, or imprisonment. This negative form of success is largely connected with groups of egotistical men blinded by imaginary boundaries, such as people associated with gangs, mafias, Klans, and cults, basically people who cannot think for themselves.

Such individuals have a desire to succeed, yet they have a mind fueled by negative thoughts and intentions. This lifestyle has no happy ending with the exception of those that can transmit their negative thoughts to a more positive nature.

Analyze history and the present and you will discover that when herds of men unite, it is usually in attempt to obtain un-authentic power. When societies gather and combine negative thoughts and intentions, man will be driven to do just about anything for that cause, which was the case in the 911 terrorist attacks and the January 6th insurrection. The problem with our minds is that they are capable of believing in thoughts and causes, whether they are positive or negative, moreover, we are willing to die for these thoughts, even if they are a lie or untrue.

Thousands of people went on January 6th because their leader called upon them via social media; some died that day protecting the integrity of democracy, others died because they believed in the big lie. Think about this, because one person lost an election and could not do the right thing and concede like other politicians do when they lose; that one person succeeded in causing so much division within us, which led to numerous deaths on Jan 6th. This is a prime example of <u>negative</u> success!

It upsets me when we have racist politicians wanting those who attacked the capitol to be released and/or treated better in prison. They complain how unfair it is that there was no justice done towards those from Black Lives Matter who protested in the streets for injustice, even though there was. However, those protests were held in lieu of hundreds of years of discrimination and prejudice towards the African Americans in this country. What happened on January 6th was complete opposite of that; it was an attack on democracy and all the progress that we have made thus far, all because one person cannot tell the truth.

From the words of another racist monster, Adolf Hitler once said, "If you tell a big enough lie and tell it frequently enough, it will be believed." Well, it was believed by half of America and this lie has crippled and corrupted us to our core.

It is odd that even in these days, prejudice herds like the KKK, the Oath Keeps, Proud Boys and The Three Percenters are allowed to tour America's cities, gathering and recruiting members at our local courthouses. If people of color did this or would have done the exact same thing that was done on January 6th, it would have been escalated to a slaughtering of colored people. That is the America we are living in today.

Hate groups like this teach their members to hate, to fear, to be biased towards others who are not white. The agenda is to make America great again by supporting white supremacy and/or white evangelicals. As you can see groups like this seemed to have been fading away, only to re-flourish in 2016 for some odd reason.

They feed off the minds of the weak. These blinded individuals can be easily controlled and taught to believe in a cause, even if it is wrong and erratic. These blinded humans can then translate into reality, the negative thought impulses of desire, such as acts of harassment, hate, racism, and even murder. These racist domestic terrorist groups or individuals can bring forth a lifetime of negativity and destruction, and the worst part as they will see no wrongdoing on their part. As Trump said, "they are good people."

This form of success is negative and many politicians on the right share this mindset. It is this negative mindset called racism that we the people have been trying to eliminate for so long now, because it is dangerous and it causes pain and suffering.

It is minds blinded by imaginary boundaries that lead humans to hate and acts of war. Evidence to support this is that at any given time, there are as many as <u>forty</u> wars being fought on earth. These herds of men gather in attempt to kill and make hell for one another over their beliefs and opinions. Together they destroy love and nature; furthermore, each war brings forth with it the possibility of total self-destruction. Any heard of men, killing another herd of men, is blind to see that we are all from the same heard, just different labels.

Today, many of established societies attempt desperately to purify America into one single race and/or faith. They chant, build the wall, or they are taking our jobs, and they are replacing us. They want to separate families who are seeking asylum and a better life. They say, we don't care if they come in, just do it like our relatives did, legally, not realizing how relentlessly difficult we have made it for immigrants to come through legally. This is why so many cross illegally and unfortunately many die. I know that they will try and change this dismay in history books in the future, just like they don't want to teach our children the truth now, about our American history and slavery.

Here is the truth, even if you were to have a nation that was all one single race, like the white race, or one religion, like Christianity; a pure race nation would continue to produce both positive and negative actions, heroes and criminals. Although it may seem that certain races are at fault for the earth's problems; the only race to truly blame is the human race. That so-called pure-race has long gone by, so now it is time to enjoy the dissolving of imaginary boundaries and appreciate the blending of human cultures and races everywhere.

If humans are to succeed in existing, we must concentrate on living and what we can do to improve life. We must close our minds to the negative minds that believe and encourage the end of time. The end of time is a negative thought that the subconscious minds of humans have transited into reality - the means in which we are now capable of destroying earth, not just one way, but two ways and more ways will come if we do not change our consciousness. If we are to continue to exist, our universal mind (Infinite Intelligence) must receive humanities desire to exist. Another words positive thinking and affirmations of our love for life and adoration for the higher power – Mother Nature.

By far the highest value of success humans can attain as a whole is to succeed in breaking through the imaginary boundaries of the mind. If this success is reached all other successes are possible, thereafter. A mind that desires the end of time is a mind filled with fear and negativity. Sadly, these minds are everywhere, anticipating the end, they are waiting to reunite with lost loved ones in a better place, never comprehending that the better place is here on earth, right now.

I know this may be hard to comprehend, but the people we have lost in our lives are here on earth, reincarnated and living again amongst us. This is why it is so crucial to make earth better each life.

If you really love your lost ones, pray that they are living the best new life possible in their subsequent life. Send love and blessing to them. I often pray for my lost ones who have passed away and ask the universe to bless them whether they are still in the intangible state awaiting to be reborn or if they are reborn again. I ask that they have a wonderful, loving upbringing and that they be protected from all harm, especially sexual predators and murderers. Please understand that if we do nothing to make life better, but are merely passing through as they say, then we have wasted the purpose of life. Each time we are reborn, we are born into a different family, culture, ethnicity, etc., so it is crucial that we eliminate racism and embrace the fact that we are all one.

We also need to start to value the real things in life like nature and the sun; the actual entities that allow us to exist and sustain life. Mother Nature provides water for us, she provides the elements needed to shelter us and she nourishes us through our entire lifetime with foods, and water; yet most of us do not even acknowledge her, much less appreciate her. Not many show her love, respect and honor.

The sun is located 93 million miles away from us, it is so precious, because it is the true light of the world and warms our bodies and gives life to all things; yet we give no reverence to the sun. For way too long, humans have praised and worshipped the wrong Father and Son completely, simply because we are stuck believing that a certain belief system is the absolute truth. Show that devotion to the actual entities that allow you to be alive and made you; namely, the universe, Mother Nature, and the Sun! This is the _real_ holy trinity, because without any of these three, there is no _life_ and there is no you!

Religious leaders stand in front of their money givers each week and preach that the end is near and that it is a good thing, for Jesus is coming to judge the living and the dead. This instills fear in the herd, which enables such mega-church leaders to exploit the herd and derail them from their true purpose.

Understand that most religious leaders are trying to succeed just like anyone else, and humanity has made many of them multi-millionaires some billionaires. And while numerous religious leaders succeed financially, they do very little to save the earth and nature, nor help the hands that feed them. Saving earth requires no money, just love. Not a love for power, money, or greed, but instead, a love for life.

We have developed the means of blinding each other for our own financial gain. If you truly desire money or success, do what you love, and true success will find you. If you desire spirituality, seek within. No mega worshipping venue, service or televangelist can bring you closer to the infinite spirit that created you, than you can; by living in the moment and being on your true path and being true to yourself.

All in all, there are no short cuts to success; many will blind you into believing differently, however if you attempt to cheat success, you shall meet failure. To win, succeed, or triumph in any walk of life, you must have faith in your step. No pep in the step, no success. Those that choose to become successful by cheating, scamming, lying, and condescending others are those that will prolong the suffering and blindness of humanity. Avoid this type of success and you have already succeeded!

> I've come to believe that each of us
> has a personal calling that's as unique
> as a fingerprint – and that the
> best way to succeed is to discover what you
> love and then find a way to offer it
> to others in the form of service, working
> hard, and also allowing the energy of
> the universe to lead you.
>
> - Oprah Winfrey

(84)

<u>**-Keys to Success-**</u>

Throughout the previous chapters, we have covered the field of success. For if we are to survive, we must learn how to succeed. This topic is a favorite within each of us because it is based upon our emotions, thoughts, desires, and destiny. Everyone has their interpretation of success, so what I am going to reveal is how to become successful in your own purpose.

Abraham Lincoln writes, "Always bear in mind that your own resolution to success is more important than any other one thing." Ralph Waldo Emerson presented his view on what success was to him in the following, "To laugh often and much; to win the respect of intelligent people and the affection of children, to earn the appreciation of honest critics and endure the betrayal of false friends; to appreciate beauty, to find the best in others; to leave the world a bit better, whether by a healthy child, a garden patch or redeemed social condition; to know even one life has breathed easier because you have lived. This is to have succeeded."

There are countless configurations given to the meaning of success. What does success mean to you? Write it down somewhere, this allows the subconscious mind to translate it into reality even more so. In this magic lies the secret to success. The secret is no secret at all, it's common sense and explained perfectly by Mr. Hill in four simple steps.

1. A definite purpose backed by a burning desire for its fulfillment.
2. A definite plan, expressed in continuous action.
3. A mind closed tightly against all negative and discouraging influences, including suggestions of relatives, friends, and acquaintances.
4. A friendly alliance with one or more persons who will encourage one to follow through with both plan and purpose.

The first step towards success requires a purpose, if you do not feel that you have a purpose in your life, you will affect, envy and/or latch on to another person's purpose. It is these individuals who never find their purpose that contribute very little or nothing at all to humanity and the wellbeing of the earth. Your purpose in life is what you love, it's what you specialize in, it is your natural gift. I wrote this very book in 1996 when I was just 19 years old, I put it on shelf and begin pursuing what I thought was success. I spent most of my life chasing "the dream", when I got it, it wasn't what I thought. My dream or purpose was right in front of me all along, but I allowed myself to be distracted for thirty years. I always knew I was a writer, but I didn't believe in my younger self.

When I write, I feel so alive; it's as if time passes by so quickly, because I am doing what my soul was meant to be doing. I am connected to my soul's code or purpose, and I realized that the information that my soul has collected over my existences is what I needed to express to help heal this country and this world. This was my gift, to see the world in reality and to help others see beyond the things that blind us and divide us.

I often debate with a relative of mine, who sides with the right and believes he is always right. It's a clear line down the middle, and he believes that more guns are the answer, and that abortion should be up to male political leaders of this world and not women. That African American athletes should <u>not</u> kneel in protest during the Star Spangle Banner song, and that Trump should finish that wall of division and that global warming is a hoax, just like Covid.

After long heated debates, I often remind him that being on the right side does not make him right. And while I don't label myself as anything other than a human, I know in my heart that we are all different and because I love him, I have to forgive him for being so unaware and so misinformed, to put it politely. I've realized that here is person who has never really self-educated himself yet knows it all.

I have to remind myself that I know that I am on the right side of history, and I pray that one day people like my dear cousin will awaken to the universal truths, educate themselves and open their eyes. But the chances of this happening are very slim to none, that is because nature created us to be unique individuals and people like him suffer from intolerance.

We each possess our own personality traits, our own views, and our own preferences. Each of us has a distinctive mind, a magnificent mind that helps us shape who we are. I always tell him thank God that we are all different, because if we all thought the same, listened to same music, ate the same things, and believed in the same things, this world would not be the wonderful diverse world that it is today.

It would be quite boring to be honest; if every human were the exact same. I love the fact that we are all different and I respect and admire everyone's life and opinion. We must let go and stop trying to make everyone we meet conformed into what we want them to be; this is especially true to my evangelical brothers who mean well, I'm sure, but are so desperate, it's annoying. It was Jesus who clearly said that his greatest command was to love God with all your heart and Love your neighbor, as yourself.

To truly love yourself and your neighbor is to stop harassing people at gay pride events, and to stop hating on immigrants, or women who are fighting for their rights again. It's to stop trying to suppress voters with your ridiculous rezoning's and ultimately; to stop hating on all religions that are not yours. Instead try using that energy to stop gun violence, racist militias, and those who are destroying nature and our democracy with their big lies and stupidity.

Every person has a purpose in life; unfortunately, not all will find theirs, thanks to the complexities of our made-up imaginary boundaries and to drug and alcohol abuse. If you are one who is currently unhappy or unsatisfied with your profession, then you have clung on to another person's purpose in life, meaning you are working to help their idea flourish. It is essential to find your soul's purpose, or you will find that nothing in life is worthwhile, even if you are successful and wealthy. Success will feel empty if it is not your true passion.

Charles Kingsley describes it best when he stated: "We act as though comfort and luxury were the chief requirements of life, when all that we need to make us happy is something to be enthusiastic about." Billions of people will go through life in search of the comfort zone; such individuals make that their purpose, neglecting their true purpose in life. I know because I fell into this trap too.

In their search for the comfort zone, most married couples in America are trained to work outside of their home, accumulating mass wealth for someone else's ideas other than their own. Unfortunately, many parents are forced to choose careers over raising their children. It has been said that being a parent is the most significant job that there is, yet millions of Americans are robed from this job, and just like in the wild, if the parent is not present, the child is more susceptible to be preyed upon and/or distracted from their true purpose.

People who feel that they have no relevant purpose in life will not succeed past the comfort zone. The comfort zone is the imaginary web in which humans from all parts of the world compete and get caught up in. Hence the phrase; "Keeping up with the Joneses." Their purpose is to rise above poverty yet sink just below true success.

These are those individuals who work most of their life, if not all, at places of employment disliked or tolerated just because. They are the modern-day slaves of this country, only these hard workers earn minimum wage and above. All political and religious societies and their affiliates need these laborers to continue working, so that they can continue to collect *mass wealth*. It is a system that we have created where we are taught not to look for that needle in the haystack, but instead to search for the comfort zone. Like crabs in a crab trap, we stay stuck in this pattern that prevents us from reaching our true purpose and living our optimal life!

True success requires a purpose, true purpose requires a search. They blind you from searching, however, the search is within and only there can one find true purpose and happiness. You have to take some time with yourself away from all distractions and study the synchronicity of your life by recalling on your childhood. The questions you must ask are, what have I always been good at? What comes naturally to me? What do I love to do? How can I contribute to making this world a better place?

If you cannot pinpoint your purpose right away, be patient, but be persistent. Become one with nature and engulf yourself in her beautiful surroundings and ask her to allow yourself to fulfill your purpose. Meditate, manifest, and follow your heart and you will flow and grow into your destiny, for she will guide you through synchronicity.

I must warn you though; one of the most common causes of failure is indecision. Decide what your purpose is or what you love to do and do not allow others to discourage you in any way, especially friends and family. Sometimes they are the crabs holding us down.

Choose your strongest ability, in which confidence comes naturally; blend it with faith, and you will live with purpose and live to your full potential and more importantly; you will find inner peace. Remember those most negative and envious towards your purpose are like that because they cannot find theirs. Perhaps the most common weakness of humans is to leave their mind open to the influence of negative, destructive and/or narrow-minded people. This negative energy is transferred through opinions, ridicule, and discrimination. Do not allow anyone to control your mind, it is yours!

When you find your life's purpose, protect it, for others will attempt to rob it from you and/or not allow you to achieve it. Do not brag to others about what you are going to do or about your desires, transfer them first into reality and allow your ideas, thoughts, and purposes to speak louder than words. Deeds and not words are what counts most in the pursuit of happiness and success.

Many times, the negative opinions of others will destroy your ability to achieve your intended goals. Do not play the fool, for it is those whom you allow into your life that are the grand creators of negativity and envy. Someone who has no knowledge of you is not really seeking to destroy you or take you down. It is often those we allow into our lives that truly envy and despise you. Sadly, it can often be family members and/or close friends that envy and derail you off of your true path, if so, get back on there and do not allow others to think for you, you have a mind of your own, use it!

If you recognize ridicule or mental harassment incoming from others, remember that such individuals are attempting to drain you, for they do not know that nature is humanity's power source and not you. Nature provides you with a scull to protect your brain, but it is your responsibility to build a wall in your mind that will not tolerate negative or destructive suggestions and opinions from others. When you are done building this wall, label it as your *willpower*, because that is what it is. This guardian protects against negativity from entering and destroying your chances of productivity, creativity, success, and love.

The saddest decision one can partake in is to hate, hold a grudge, or not forgive people who have offended you. Diseases emerge from such feelings and emotions. Let it go, let God or whatever you believe in deal with it. Nothing in life is worth stressing over; stress is nothing more than people thinking stressful thoughts. You now know that you have the power to influence your mind and turn those negative thoughts into positive thoughts, if you don't, the subconscious mind will translate more stress into your life.

Human minds can be powerful intangible weapons, equipped with poison arrows. These poison arrows are nothing more than bad vibes being sent from one mind to another. They transport such negative forces that humans with weak minds can develop in their life mishaps or in extreme cases inexplicable diseases and even death.

Each individual has the potential to send or pass on negative suggestions or impulses of energy to others. Some refer to this as witchcraft, placing spells, or voodoo; but these people can be anywhere, because everyone possesses the power to send and receive telepathically and subconsciously.

A mind that uses its powers to harm others is a mind that can only prey upon those of little or no will power, such minds do not believe in karma, but rest assured, it will come back to them. These are those who have no love for their neighbor, nor themselves.

All the known battles of the world began in the minds of people blinded by imaginary boundaries. These minds have the ability to seek the purpose of life, but instead choose to destroy it. From this moment on, vow to listen within or you shall forever struggle for power like them. Reach a firm decision to avoid all who depress you, discourage you or try to bring you down. These people are those who cannot rise above it, themselves and so they will attempt to bring you down.

High self-esteem and a strong willpower create confidence; faith and confidence exert triumph. If they say you can't succeed prove them wrong, if they say that your idea is crazy, prove them crazy. Make the decision to surround yourself with people who do not drain you or distract you. When a mosquito is sucking the blood out of you, you do not do nothing. Likewise, when a person is draining you of your energy, you must call out these people and let them know that you are not giving away your energy, nor tolerating their negativity.

Mother Nature has an endless supply of energy for those fortunate enough to acknowledge her. Step up and call them out, tell them that you do not like the way that you are being treated and if they do not respect you or your position, then you do not need them in your life; good riddance!

Through the aid of creative imagination, one can find his or her true calling, for only there can one connect with the divine energy in which created them. Failure to use this faculty of the subconscious mind will result in the calling from others and your purpose in life becomes listening to them and not within.

Anything you can conceive and believe, you can achieve. Many use the S.P.E.C method, Select it, Project it, Expect it, Collect it. All who have succeeded in life can validate truth to this formula. The only limitations are those we give power to. All who have found and fulfilled themselves through purpose and passion have protected themselves from the negativities that I warn you of. The people who have succeeded in life not only believed in their ideas, plans and thoughts, but they translated them into existence, so that life can somehow benefit as well.

All who have succeeded, have struggled, suffered, or experience some form of adversity along the way to reaching their goals. Those who succeed are those who persevere, against all odds. Persist, not prolong, your purpose, goals, and ambitions and you my friend will be on track to living your optimal life; moreover, you will become the light for others to succeed in their journey.

I often say that you cannot keep two things in life down and that is true love and true purpose/talent. To help reach your resolution of success was the design of this chapter. Fulfilled, self-confident, whole-hearted, creative human beings, is what is going to save humanity. You, the reader, now know things that other humans cannot comprehend.

I believe, collectively and over time, we will possess the ultimate power to succeed as a whole beyond this and other millenniums to come. However, let us not forget that all of the other types of humans that we have shared earth with are now extinct.

It is time to consciously unite as a human species and do what is necessary, so that success will have meaning for future beings. The day we live free from all imaginary boundaries is the day we succeed in controlling the direction we are headed. Our global destiny lies in our thoughts, then in our hands. Without further due, let the healing begin....

-<u>Natural Healing</u>-

Visualize a planet of peace and harmony, a place where all respected and treated each other equally. Simply imagine it, it is your right. If you cannot imagine it, then you remain blinded by imaginary boundaries and must become one with nature. Store that thought and now enter the realm of reality. To become one with nature one protects, respects, and honors her all the time. Every <u>minute</u> of every day an area the size of forty football fields is being destroyed by humanity and/or by the effects of global warming and deforestation.

We, the human species, allow rich companies to enter the earth's forest that do not belong to us and destroy nature that sustains life. Forest that absorb carbon dioxide and produces something we need to survive, oxygen. This global crime is completely ignored, for they believe that it has no immediate effect on us now, and that it will eventually grow back. Sadly enough, these hundred-year-old trees will not grow back quickly enough if they can grow back at all, through the erosion, and/or through the clearing for farmland. Because of countries like America, (especially America) our natural rain forest of this wondrous world are perishing.

Money hungry leaders are leading humanity to the termination of that which sustains life for this planet – the atmosphere; mother nature's willpower. If there is no forest, then there is no ozone layer, no ozone layer, no life. Get it? Good, because we are running out of time staying blinded and pretending not to see the real crimes at hand.

One solution to global warming is about to be revealed but before anyone can judge this solution, one must learn it's significance in human evolution. This solution is known and used worldwide to help relieve the pain caused by arthritis and rheumatism; the same solution reduces inter-ocular pressure and prevents the advances of glaucoma, a disease that blinds roughly three million people in America and is the second leading cause of blindness worldwide.

This solution is used to treat digestive disorders, neuralgia, insomnia, depression, stress, migraine headaches and inflammation. In addition, it reduces spastics in multiple sclerosis and paralysis, including paraplegia, quadriplegia, and muscular dystrophy. If that is not enough; it is used to help emphysema and asthma patients breathe more freely. It is also used to prevent epileptic seizures, to relieve chronic pain of spinal-bifid, muscular spasm and those who suffer from other spinal injuries.

It has also been successful in treating dysentery, uterine hemorrhage, palsy, anthrax, blood poisoning, incontinence, leprosy, snake bites, tonsillitis, parasites, and legions of other medical uses much too long for description. For women, it was once nature's gift to help facilitate childbirth, stimulate lactation, and reduce the pain of menstrual cramping.

It eases the withdraws from alcohol and nicotine addiction and other deadly man-made drugs. Perhaps its most significant role is its ability to help fellow humans suffering from terminal illness, such as the Aids and cancer patients who undergo hard-to-tolerate medications, such as chemotherapy. This solution is key to their health and longevity.

It is also key in maximizing the ability to harness the faculty of creative imagination. Humans have produced shoes, laces, handbags, bracelets, necklaces, hats, jeans, towels, diapers, baby clothing and casual clothing for adults, such as Ralph Loren. Powders, perfumes, skin creams, shampoos, lip balm, salves and numerous cosmetics and detergents have been made through this solution.

While it is used to create beauty products, it is also used to create houses, for this solution is superior to wood in all aspects. It can also be made into a material similar to fiber glass. The infamous Henry Ford took this solution and ingeniously created and operated the very first automobile of its kind. He then used the same solution to create a fuel, making this one of the most highly productive, all natural automobiles to ever be produced!

If you still remain unaware of what the solution is, you must comprehend that this solution is natural but branded by those blinded by imaginary boundaries as harmful, illegal, and evil, blocking it from its potential and medicinal capabilities. And while many states are starting to see the benefits of this solution and relaxing their laws, still many states are criminalizing and criticizing over it.

(93)

Together, modern day politicians and many bible believers have repressed her and blame her for the causing of violence and ignorance. When in fact, it is these societies and their laws that cause the real dangers.

Many bible believers believe the word of the lord has been perverted through the ages, I believe vice versa. The word of the Lord came into this world perverted and now they are trying desperately to keep it alive through translations and interpretations of a positive God, who is all loving.

If anything, this solution has been corrupted and despised by those whom have done nothing for the earth because they are merely passing through, and ironically it is this solution that is going to cover their you know what, as our world fully awakens and deviates from their so-called revelations.

If we could see
the miracle of a
single flower
clearly, our
whole life
would change!

Buddha

-<u>Noumenon</u>-

In the bible (Genesis 1:11) "Then God said, let the earth bring forth grass, the herb that yields seed and the fruit tree that yields fruit according to its kind whose seed is in itself, on the earth." Then in chapter two, the authors of the bible described the tree of knowledge as an apple tree and the devil transforms into a talking snake and persuades guess who, not Adam but Eve to eat from the forbidden fruit.

Why would an all-knowing God, first of all create an angel that would one day betray him and become the devil; secondly create a tree that would cause humans to be God-like and knowing good and evil if he did want us be God-like? In all loving God would not do this deceit to humanity but a human with limited knowledge would use this story to captivate and capture the minds of billions of people. Today there is a new tree of knowledge and bible believers all around the world are being taught to stay away from.

Religious leaders discriminate against this solution for they fear its potential and they should fear it! They do not fear so much its material transformation, instead they fear its spiritual transformation and its ability to see right passed all the corruption and delusions. This modern-day tree of knowledge is labeled as a product of the devil by most religious societies; but in reality, it is proving to be a major contributor to our salvation from self-destruction and global warming. It is a plant that opens eyes and expands minds everywhere around the world and helps us recognize the God within us.

Labeled as Cannabis sativa, hemp, or marijuana, this healing plant of nature is the solution to help control violence, human suffering and most importantly, the global erosion caused by humans.

It is said that hemp was first cultivated and used around 10,000 BCE in ancient Chinese civilizations; it was used for food, fiber, and medicine. The Greeks, Romans, Egyptians, Hittites, and Scythians used hemp in their daily lives for medicine, recreation, and religious purposes. It spread to several Mediterranean Countries in Europe in the early Christian era through the Middle Ages, then brought over to the US by English settlers in 1606.

(95)

This prolific plant was created by Mother Nature for a purpose and through that purpose, sparked the ingredients needed to begin the awakening process. Here is the real tree of knowledge because it has assisted in bringing out the very best creative energy within us.

Mother Nature first produced this magical plant about 28 million years ago in eastern Tibetan according to a pollen study. Please push away your judgements and opinions of hemp for just a moment, as we learn what this plant has meant and done for our evolution. You might be surprised!

From "THE GREAT BOOK OF HEMP" Ehud C Sperling writes; "When Gutenberg's presses started rolling, it was hemp paper that received the ink and spread the word of the bible to an awakening Europe. When the urge to find a new world, a new way of living, gave rise to the age of discovery, some 500 years ago, it was hemp that powered this urge, giving the explorers the sails and courage needed to cross oceans.

When it came time to define this new world, it's goals and aspirations, it was hemp paper that the original drafts of the United States Constitution and Declaration of Independence were written on. As the young nation moved west it was hemp that covered the settler's wagons.

During World War I, when supplies of raw fiber were cut off by the Japanese, hemp was reintroduced to the US farmer to support the war effort, as the US Department of Agriculture proclaimed, "Hemp for Victory". Hemp - A message of receptors in the human brain waiting to receive its biochemical messages. A message of respect for earth, its plants, and animals, for our bodies and food we ate, for cultures and people other than our own was heard and the sea of change it brought is still being played out today!"

From the first books of the bible to the first drafts of the US Constitution, hemp has played a huge roll in human evolution and creative progression. Everybody has an opinion of hemp, most of which is negative because of the religious and political views, but few know the actual know the facts.

In 1937, the marijuana tax prohibited the use, sale, and cultivation of all marijuana in the US. In a time of need, which was just five years later, during the World War II, the U.S Department of Agriculture promoted American farmers to grow hemp in abundance for war effort. Thus, over 150,000 acres of hemp were planted in 1943, to heal and surpass Americans over such calamity; it was used to make uniforms and rope that would sustain the elements of war. Ultimately alcohol and tobacco became accepted in society, while hemp became illegal and classified thereafter as a gateway drug to harder drugs.

Because of political and religious bias, millions of Americans have been arrested on marijuana charges. This occurs because politicians and religious leaders are aware that this plant enables humans to perceive the world differently. It is a dose of reality with the power to eliminate the strangle holds of imaginary boundaries. Bob Marley referred to hemp as "The herb that heals all nations."

The war on drugs has cost Americans trillions of dollars and wasted energy. Today there are more drugs on the streets then there were when we first started this senseless war. It is important to understand that mind stimulants have always been around and will always be around, as long as there is a demand.

Trade and selling are the fundamentals that sparked civilization. Getting together and feeling certain substances is a natural process that goes back to the beginning of time. What we have to do is realize that marijuana is the least harmful of the many drugs that out there. Never before have we seen so many people on the streets talking and/or fighting with themselves. When we have meth addicts, opiate addicts, alcoholics, pill poppers, synthetic drug users; all living on the streets or close to it, we have failed as a society.

We are creating so many mental health issues, it is pathetic. How can anyone look up to us in the world, and aspire to be like us, when we are the land of the living zombies. We enrich so many other countries yet neglect ourselves. Children that are neglected are those most prone to harm, violence, and troubled paths. Just as governments who neglect their countries, we are headed down a path of destruction. The kind of power that America displays to the world is not authentic, which will lead to ongoing violence, wars and more terrorist attacks.

(97)

We the people must transform our power, not to where the world fears us, but aspires to be like us. Most right wingers are led by ego and fear, and do not allow us to reach our full potential. A true leader will lead by example and not by trying to instill fear in others. They understand that leading is not about them, but about those that they serve. True leaders are filled with inclusiveness and would not divide us, nor try to destroy the integrity of our Country.

The religious right attempts to intertwine religion with politics and they keep pushing this lifestyle upon Americans, not realizing that their agenda is what causes much of this mental anguish.

Rowan Robinson writes, "The modern church of progress, which preaches survival of the fittest competition, and motivates through the promise of material wealth. Hemp's enhancement of the current moment and of empathy and independent thinking, throws this whole ideology into question. Why devote countless hours to accumulating wealth to buy a happiness and satisfaction that already thrives within each and every moment?"

A leader is best when
people barely know
he exists, when his
work is done, his aim
fulfilled, they will say:
we did it ourselves.

-Lao Tzu

(98)

-<u>The Awakening</u>-

Our founding fathers fled a place that was ruled by a strict political and religious tyranny, in hopes of a better life, and here we are; but let's take a step back into time. The real history of America democracy is as follows; on September 5th, 1774, the decision was reached to hold the first Continental Congress. Two years later during the month of January 1776, a man by the name of Thomas Paine marveled the new world with his influential pamphlet titled: "<u>COMMON SENSE</u>." His literature was based upon freedom and freedom was desired by the new colonies. His words inspired an even greater decision, one that affects us even today.

Thomas Jefferson presented the fate of America on June 28th, 1776, when the original draft of the Declaration of Independence was read before congress. This draft was fixed by a committee of five and altered to their liking, and on July 4th, 1776, Thomas Jefferson read aloud the most courageous decision to ever be placed in writing. This decision turned the hands of time and one of the most successful and most powerful nations was born – The United States of America.

By the year 1789, a true leader was emerging, a distinguished gentleman who was unanimously selected to become the very first president of The United States of America – George Washington. Today he can be found virtually anywhere in the US, on money, in museums, or on monuments; even our nation's capital has been named in his honor. No American history would be complete without the mention of George Washington, Thomas Jefferson, James Madison, and Thomas Paine. But who were these men? Aside from being some of the first presidents and influencers of America, what do these men have in common?

We're these men perfect? By no means, but all of them struggled with one thing in their time and that is the institution known as slavery. President Washington wrote about his desire to end slavery and pushed for treating slave's moral and rewarding them rather than beating and mistreating them violently. He knew that the tide would turn one day and feared that this could become an all-out race war, but the influences and imaginary boundaries (religion) of their time did not allow him to make slavery obsolete.

Thomas Jefferson felt the same way, and outlawed international slave trade while he was president. He voiced his opinion about gradually freeing all of the slaves in the United States. Even the first drafts of the Declaration of Independence condemned slavery but were later altered before finalizing it by those who felt they had a god given right to own slaves because it was written in the bible. Today the religious right would probably persecute these men; not only for trying to do the right thing and free humans from the bonds of slavery, but also for promoting the use and cultivation of hemp. Each of these men played a significant role in building this country yet let us not forget that hemp played a significant role in developing these notable characters.

It was James Madison the forth US President, who said that Hemp gave him the idea and *creativity* to design a new democratic nation, and from his creativity came the US Constitution and the US Bill of Rights. As Thomas Jefferson prepared the first drafts and the most important decision in American History onto paper, it wasn't paper made from tress of the vanishing rain forest, but rather paper processed from Dutch hemp. Thomas Jefferson extended his literature and expressed how and when one should cultivate hemp. He believed approximately two tablespoons of hemp seed was ideal per household during the planting season.

Let us not forget that it was Thomas Jefferson who stated, "Hemp is of first necessity to the wealth and protection of the Country." And as we stand Trillions of dollars in depth, it is his words that come to mind. Thomas Jefferson achieved great success through his writings and knowledge and in the year 1800, Mr. Jefferson became America's third President.

It has been said that the first and third Presidents were known to have exchanged gifts of various hemps to one another as gestures of friendship. Both men were known to dislike tobacco products and not to profound on alcohol. One thing both Presidents did cherish was there prolific hemp plantations in Virginia. George Washington appears on the most common forms of US currency, both coin and dollar. The next time you encounter his face, perhaps this statement which he declared will come to mind, "Make the most of the hemp seed, sow it everywhere," or how he described it was, "A marvelous stimulant to the imagination."

These guys grew hemp in their time because it was used to make rope, fishing nets and sail gear that would create a strong canvas, but regardless of what they say these Presidents grew hemp for medicinal and recreational purposes also.

In his personal journal, President Washington wrote, "What was done with the seed saved from the India Hemp last summer? It ought, all of it, to have been sown again; that not only a stock of seed sufficient for my own purposes might have been raised, but to have disseminated the seed to others; as it is more valuable than the common hemp." The common hemp was used to produce resourceful products; the valuable hemp helped produced the United States of America.

Thomas Paine captured all who came to know his writings – a desire for freedom. This desire enabled the first Americans to cross oceans, and he clearly knew it was only possible because of hemp, "In almost every article of defense we abound, hemp flourishes even to rankness, so that we need not want cordage." The material wealth of hemp is unmatched to other products, yesterday, today, and tomorrow.

The solution to saving our remaining forest depends upon the decision to fully harvest and legalize Hemp. The US Department of Agriculture stated that one acre of hemp can produce 4.1 times more paper than an acre of trees. Reread this sentence once again, because in it lies the key solution to help alleviate the scars of global warming and global erosion.

Henry Ford, one of the greatest pioneers in American history, once said this, "Why use up the forest which were centuries in the making and the mines which required ages to lay down, if we can get the equivalent of forest and mineral products in the annual growth of the hemp fields?" Why? Because we do not honor or appreciate nature.

Our world demands numerous products from trees and cotton; _anything_ that can be made from these two resources can be made out of hemp and far superior and quicker. We allow big companies to cut down massive trees that have lived for decades or even centuries, causing real suffering to the natives and species of those lands, many times ending life and pushing life to extinction. We allow this to occur when hemp takes no more than one hundred days to fully grow an amazing 16 feet tall.

(101)

From the Environmental and Energy Study Institute, "Cambridge University researcher Darshil Shah stated that hemp can capture between eight and 15 tons of atmospheric carbon dioxide (CO2) for each hectare of cultivation, a rate twice that of a forest. Its fast growth rate means that farmers have the opportunity to harvest hemp multiple times per year, priming it for climate mitigation efforts.

Cultivating hemp doesn't require the heavy use of pesticides or large amounts of water, and with such water-input versatility, the plant can be grown in a variety of types of soils and climates. When planted, hemp can be used as a cover crop and bolster the soil nutrient profile. The plant can also help stabilize erosion with its deep roots that also absorb and remove heavy metals from the ground.

Hemp's high yields hold the promise of replacing other fiber- and oil-producing plants. According to the National Hemp Association, one acre of hemp produces double the amount of oil than an acre of peanuts does, and it also produces four times as much fiber pulp used for paper than an acre of trees does. When processed, every part of the hemp plant can be used for a wide range of products, including biofuels and textiles.

The wide range of versatile hemp-derived products has the potential to address U.S. reliance on plastics, fossil fuels, and cotton, by serving as a sustainable replacement. Currently, the Center for International Environmental Law predicts that plastic consumption will continue increasing and account for 20 percent of oil consumption by 2050. Hemp, however, offers a naturally biodegradable alternative that can replace petroleum-based plastic materials on both the commercial and industrial scale.

Alongside bioplastics, hemp has gained prominence being a durable alternative to cotton, as it requires less land and around half of the water cotton crops need. Beyond clothing and plastics, hemp has been used in construction with products like hempcrete, and its seeds have been used in cosmetics and in food for their nutritional value. With this plethora of sustainable benefits, hemp has the potential to reshape more than just agriculture.

Moreover, the carbon sequestration of hemp has the potential to reduce greenhouse gas (GHG) emissions from U.S. agriculture—which the EPA estimated accounted for 11.2 percent of total U.S. GHG emissions in 2020. By offering sustainable alternatives to high-emission products, hemp cultivation could help the United States meet its climate goals".

Thankfully America is grasping the many uses of hemp, and we are mass cultivating it now for good reasons. It may cost some money to go green, but once we do, we are essentially saving not only trees, but life itself. As it is now, with so many natural forest fires due to the effects of global warming, combined with what humans have cut down for material gain, we need to do this for the love and safety of our planet.

Hemp is truly of first necessity, then and especially now. I cannot express enough the importance of hemp and its healing powers. If you do not comprehend its vital impact and significance on humanity, hopefully educating yourself (like you just did) on the many benefits of it will encourage you to do so, and/or at least, not be against it. If we can continue to mass harvest Hemp and it can become one of our top cash crops, America will begin to lead the way as a country that inspires the world, by displaying the many valuable uses and innovative products that can be produced out of Hemp.

Understand now that the war on drugs will never resolve. Man-made drugs are forms of energy that can steer mankind into the worst-case scenario in our evolutionary journey. Man-made stimulants lead us to our personal nemesis, for man-made drugs enable humans to no longer care about life and where our world is headed.

Those that indulge in man-made drugs are often those individuals that think wasteful thoughts and produce negative actions, resulting in wasted energy, crime, and suffering. Through the years of experimenting, very few man-made drugs have served a good purpose for a struggling humanity.

Man-made drugs have the power to kill and the power to negatively influence the life of those who are on them. Cocaine, crack, meth, heroin, and the opiate family including prescribed legal drugs that derive from opiates, Fentanyl, PCP are just some of the man-made drugs that kill our fellow humans and sadly – our youth!

These drugs are not going anywhere, because of our high demand in America and more synthetic variations will be produced in the future, because they can go easily undetected, which just keeps escalating the dangers of drugs. Never can a nation ban drugs entirely, yet it is not too late to educate the human race on the dangers of man-made and/or destructive drugs.

People are going to use drugs legally and illegally for as long as we exist, why judge over a drug that allows you to connect within to Mother Nature and allows you to generate peaceful thoughts and emotions, rather than bring out the worst in us and create zombies out of us.

I am not suggesting that everyone go get high, because it is not for <u>everyone</u>. But if we are to make it, we need to be in a good head space and if an adult MUST alter their mind; then I think it would be wise and safe to say that cannabis is the mind stimulant that we as a society should be ok with. After all, it was through this state of mind that the United States of America were born.

Someone once said that a mind of peace, a mind focused on not harming others, is stronger than any physical force in the entire universe. If this is true, then the universal mind made up of every race, culture, and every language around the world united as one under the influence of Hemp, is the most powerful mindset of all. It is the ultimate tool (state of mind) in saving humanity.

It helps humans to listen within and to see reality. Do you need hemp to see the auspicious visions that we carry within? No, not at all, many can acquire this vision without it, but in a world where our minds are so tuned out with manmade drugs and alcohol; cannabis can help humble a man and bring him into reality; moreover, it can raise his creativity levels and allow him or her to do astonishing things.

There is no other mind-stimulant in this world where one can actually read and write and retain knowledge. I know, because I wrote this entire book in this manner when I was in my youth. I no longer consume hemp, but I know that one can achieve great success and reach stupendous heights of creativity with hemp alone and not mixing it with any other substances. Perhaps the most significant component of hemp is it's profound effect on the brain, you begin to <u>imagine</u> a world of peace and love for all things, especially for Mother Nature. You see the injustices of the world.

Many humans despise hemp because they cannot resonate with this state of mind. Never comprehending that this state of mind thrives within each of us; hemp just allows certain individuals to unlock or enhance this vision, but the vision is always there, within our souls. The problem is that the imaginary boundaries in our mind that are taught to us prevent us from being able to see these auspicious visions within; hemp helps dissolve those boundaries and divisions, as does listening to your common sense. Thus, many political and religious members have tried for more than a century to ban hemp and destroy nature in the process, for they know once one becomes one with nature, he or she becomes nature's guardian for life.

No longer will one allow so-called leaders to be oppressive, destructive, or ignorant towards nature and humanity. All imaginary boundaries of the mind naturally dissolve, allowing humans to see the destructive nature of religious systems have caused. This is the real reason why hemp has this negative connotation on it, and why Presidents such as Trump and John F Kennedy are so dissimilar; polar opposites. One was filled with integrity and inhaled cannabis regularly for back pain, the other exhaled so much hatred and lies, and that our world may never recover from such deceit.

Whether you are for hemp or against it, if we do not end its reputation as being evil and illegal, that outlook can lead us to the end. I ask you then, the reader, not for your money as all of these so-called leaders do, but instead, for the simplest thing; allow mother nature to take her course, remember we are just passengers on her journey and not vice-versa.

Since the precious beginning of human existence, humans have struggled with questions such as how can we as a species live in peace? How can we disengage from war? How can we save the rain forest? The animal kingdom? The Ozone Layer? Ourselves? How can we transform this world for the better? How can we stop mass-shootings? By accepting the reality of this philosophy and putting it to great use.

Negative thoughts, negative mind stimulants, easy access to guns and the imaginary boundaries that divide us produce the crisis we are now faced with. I hope that you have learned to distinguish fantasy from reality. They will attempt to combine the two and deceive you. They will tell you to believe in this because it's true, even if it is a lie. They will attempt to keep you in the comfort zone or the herd, for their sole existence depends upon it. Always keep in mind though, that the best defense to this intolerance and ignorance is your - Common Sense and that they cannot take from you!

-<u>The Chosen Ones</u>-

The auspicious vision of freedom for all is within each of us, it was planted there by the great spirit when you were born from her spirit over 14 billion years ago. It has always been there, however if we do not use our common sense then you cannot experience it. Nothing in the universe is confined, nor should we be, we are free. Man-made mind stimulants, imaginary boundaries and our own intolerance prevent us from seeing it. The whole purpose of this literature was intended for you to open the eyes of your heart and to recognize that we are living on a beautiful thriving planet. We have the power to co-create our surroundings, shape our lives, and our planet, simply by influencing our minds.

When we die, we are merely passing through our intangible life only to return to life manifested. Everything must be born, and everything must transition. Therefore, we are like a leaf on a tree that will fall in autumn, only to be reborn again in spring. This everlasting dance between the intangible energy manifesting into tangible energy can only be described as Mother Nature's passion.

David Viscott once wrote, that "The purpose of life is to discover your gift. The work of life is to develop it. The meaning of life is to give your gift away". I am giving my gift of knowledge away to all my fellow humans through these pages, in hopes that when we are reborn again earth will return to its natural innocence and magnificent wonder with a touch of our creativity. When I think about this on a grand level; Mother Nature's gift is to create; her life's work is to sustain growth and evolution and she has given us full control of what happens to her and this amazing planet; and I hope we do the right thing!

In the previous chapters I have been pretty harsh to my fellow Christians, only because they are those most hypocritical humans on the planet. And while they're trying to save their text from the scriptures, I'm trying to save the world. They want to constantly battle for superiority and to be king of righteousness and unfortunately, they're way has gotten us here! Yet they will continue to harass and persecute anyone who does not think exactly as they do. And while I may come off as an atheist, I am not; I am just convinced that my god is a pure light, pure energy, and pure love.

Not male or female and definitely not in our image; but in a formless energy that *only* our souls can understand, because our souls come from this grand boundless spirit. Nowadays everyone's God, in all religions has evolved into the description of a loving God, which is great, because it means we are finally awakening to the fact that, the God of the Old Testament is not all loving, therefore that cannot be the actual word of God.

Whether you call your God; the universe, Shiva, Allah, Jesus, Jehovah, Krishna, Tao, infinite intelligence, Buddha, the universal mind or as I do Mother Nature, there is no right or wrong, because God is love. These are just labels we give to describe the creator of life and everything else that follows are just traditions and customs. Your soul has and will continue to be born into many of these different religions, and you will serve many Gods throughout your countless lives; but I have faith that you will at least respect other cultures and religions each time you are born because you now have this knowledge embedded in your soul.

My journey in this lifetime began in the Catholic Church. I would go to mass in an old Spanish mission church built in the 1700's with my grandmother. As I aged, I began to read everything I could that interested my soul. I have read countless books and have learned respectfully about all religions and science; which led me to question everything that I learned as a child. I've always believed in a higher power, but for me, I was just so in tune with nature that I realized, we humans cannot live without her.

I also thought of how we humans assume that God is in control of the weather, unless there is a major catastrophe like a hurricane, or a tornado; then all of a sudden, he is not in control, we shift the blame to mother nature. Understand that Mother Nature is constantly creating. This is what she does; it is her purpose to constantly create. Yet we, the most intelligent species on earth, cannot see that we are a pattern of energy that she also created. This is because the bible teaches us opposite, that she was created for us.

This led me to begin to question even more things; so, I picked up an old bible that my grandmother had, and I read it from start to finish. This bible was not watered down to show only kindness and love, (as they are nowadays) and if you want to remain a devoted Christian, please do NOT do the same thing. What I found was disturbing and vulgar and I realized that this is not a God of love, nor the word of God.

This was a book written by people from all different eras who heard stories and tales that were passed down and eventually composed into the word of God. I thought to myself if this is God's word, the absolute truth, and then I cannot believe in a God that would command killings, rapes and condone slavery. I then wrote my book in the late 90's and lived an atheist life.

Then in 2016, I had everything that money could buy, I had a remarkable career as a senior supervisor for a well-known tech company. I drove nice cars and owned my own home. Me and my high school sweetheart had three wonderful boys and we seemed to have it all. Then just like that, I almost lost it all, because I was not faithful to my wife. This devastated our family and she had made plans to leave to her mother's home with my boys that weekend. This was the saddest day of my life because I was losing my family, and all of this was my fault. How could I let myself get so distracted with society, drugs and alcohol. How could I write this book and not take my own advice.

Then on that same day (out of nowhere) one of my best friends showed up at my door and asked me if I would like to go on a retreat with him that weekend, I said no. I'm going through all of these problems right now; I told him my wife is leaving me this weekend. He said, "Then what do you have to do, sit here and sulk alone?" I told him, I don't even believe in that stuff. He said, "I went through the same thing with my wife, same situation and look at us now." I said she forgave you. He said, "No but I asked God to forgive me and made peace with him and that changed everything for me."

In 2016, I went on my first ACTS retreat; I went with the mentality that I will show these men that God does not exist; instead, they showed me nothing but love and I cried more than I have ever cried in my life. I thought of all the selfish things that I had done and put my family through. This was a full circle moment for me because I came back to the Catholic Church where I used to go with my grandmother when I was a child. This is where I feel most at home, this is my community, this is my culture, this is where I belong.

Do I agree with everything that is in the bible, absolutely not! But I realized then how the universe, God and Mother Nature were all the same things, just worded differently; but it's all about the energies that we evoke in the universe and ultimately, it's about finding Love. We have to love ourselves, so that we can fully love others.

From that retreat, I understood clearly what my purpose was in this world; it is to teach _acceptance_ of all human beings regardless of their skin color, religion, culture, ethnicity, gender, political party, nation, sexual preference, etc. I also realized that there is still a lot of judgement and hate in religion and that is because religions cannot see all as one.

My purpose has been laid out in these pages and it is to show humanity how to view all people as one. I know my purpose is _not_ to destroy religion, but rather it is to bring them all together; to take the best attributes of all the religions, creeds, customs and to show humanity that no one entity has right, even though they think they do.

Like the description of God being formless from Islam, or the reincarnation known as samsara from the Hindus or karma from the Buddhist, each religion has a piece of the puzzle, and one cannot build the puzzle alone. My purpose is to spread the message that whoever your God is, it's ok, as long as you accept the love of the creator in your heart and as long as you show love to everyone, then we are headed in the right direction. I can go into any church and show respect to their customs and traditions, without draining or trying to covert anyone; but still praying to the universe and Mother Nature in my heart. That is how confident I am in what I believe and what I know to be true. I also pray to Jesus and ask him to help me be more like him and less like the Christians who judge and hate others.

When Jesus said that "I am the way, the truth and the life," he is stating that he represents love, and he wanted us to follow love in life. Love is the way and the truth and it is the only way that we can view the auspicious visions that we carry within us. Heaven is here, we just close off the possibility and make it hell for each other. And while I know that my God has done amazing things in my life, I also know that other Gods can do those same wonderful things in other people's lives. And because I know within my soul, that God is really the universe and the subconscious mind at work; I can appreciate all Gods, all religions, and all traditions, because essentially God is within each of us, so celebrate the _divinity_ within you and understand that you are God!

I don't believe that the bible represents the _absolute_ truth in so many ways that I have shared with you throughout this book, but I understand that all religions are trying to get to the same conclusion, and that is that we are a product of _love_. Practice the religion that you feel most comfortable with and do not allow others to tell you who or what to believe in; and if you don't believe that's ok too, just live life with love and compassion. That is the key; it has always been the key! The human species has loved and expressed emotions for tens of thousands of years prior to us creating any Gods or religions. History shows us that we can live without the bible, but don't live without love!

Jesus was the most famous of the chosen ones; he was killed for spreading the message that was written in his heart. There are some scriptures that did not make it into the bible, because it paints a different picture from the creations that Moses proposes; but still, these are said to be the words of Jesus Christ, just like those of the New Testament.

In the Secret Book of John, Jesus describes the creator in the following, "She, [the first] power, the glory of Barbelo, the perfect glory among the aeons, the glory of revelation, she glorified and praised the Virgin spirt, for because of the spirit (8) she had come forth. She is the first Thought, the image of the spirit, she became the universal womb, for she precedes everything, the mother-father." Jesus knew that Mother Nature was our creator and that she is a part of the greater spirt that we now know as the universe, (God) however, in his time, the words had not been formulated to describe this yet, but that did not stop him from trying. That is powerful, because if you believe in Christ then it shows that everything written in the bible is not true.

I understand that not everything in the bible is truth or even reality and there are so many interpretations of the bible, but there is some great inspiration in it also, like in 1 Corinthians 13, "Love is patient, love is kind. It does not boast, it is not proud. It does not dishonor others, it is self-seeking, it is not easily angered and keeps no record of wrongs."

That middle line, love does not dishonor others. That line should become the model for all humanity, because if you really love someone, you will not dishonor them, nor try to own them or overpower them in any way. You would simply love them as they are, and not how you want them to be. When you have love in your heart, you will see the divinity in all things, just as they are. Let us explore now the other chosen ones who carried these auspicious visions within them and who also delivered the message that was written in their hearts.

-<u>The Auspicious Prophecy</u>-

Let's go back in time to when the battle of slavery came to halt and one of Americas most admired individuals began serving his country. He spent his lifetime searching for his calling, not realizing that his calling would be heard by everyone around the world through life spans. He, like Jesus believed in the equality and freedom for all; thus, he rose against the racist bible belt of his time and changed American history forever.

The Emancipation Proclamation and the Gettysburg Address help define this respected national figure. Lincoln played a major role in abolishing slavery, a horrible custom that the authors of the bible never attempted to do away with, even though it was wrong. This president also had the vision to want to see a country that was free. He envisioned this in a time when so many were blinded by the imaginary boundaries of the mind; hence this sparked the Civil War.

One side wanted to make slaves free, while the others believed it was their God given right to own and mistreat humans. Slave owners would even show and teach slaves scriptures from the bible, showing God's command, in order to manipulate them and keep them blinded. This would be one of the most brutal imaginary boundaries to overcome in human history and proof that humans can and will believe anything, even if it is inaccurate, but eventually the truth shall emerge and set us free.

John Wilkes Booth was a white man who grew up in the south in a slave-owning family. He was against the historical movement of freeing the slaves, and once expressed his extreme views as, "So help me holy God! My soul, life and possessions are for the South!" Then one night on April 14, 1865, Booth (an actor) slipped into the Presidential Box of then President Abraham Lincoln during the third act of a play and point-blank shot him in the head. Even though Booth took the life of the 16th president, he couldn't take the President's auspicious visions, which led to the freeing of salves. Unfortunately, we were left with the residue of racism.

From the 16th President to the 35th President of the United States. John F Kennedy, also known as JFK, once said that "A man may die, nations may rise and fall, but an idea lives on." President Kennedy had the vision too, and in a very dark time in America, when the white nationalist insisted in racial separation in the 50's and 60's. When the

(111)

KKK would lynch black people and get away with it, simply because they influenced and financed racist politicians. When black people had to sit in the back of busses and be treated like animals. When restaurants and stores would deny them service; when African Americans could not even drink water from the same fountains or use the same restrooms.

When 45 shouts "Make America Great Again," wake up! Because this is what he is trying to take us back to and we cannot go backwards. From the 46th Presidential Inauguration emerged a magnificent poet with a powerful message; here is a sample of her creative brilliance, written by Amanda Gorman, titled "The Hill We Climb."

Somehow we've weathered and witnessed
a nation that isn't broken
but simply unfinished.
We, the successors of a country and a time
where a skinny Black girl
descended from slaves and raised by a single mother
can dream of becoming president
only to find herself reciting for one.
And yes, we are far from polished,
far from pristine,
but that doesn't mean we are
striving to form a union that is perfect.
We are striving to forge a union with purpose,
to compose a country committed to all cultures, colors, characters, and
conditions of man.
And so we lift our gazes not to what stands between us
but what stands before us.
We close the divide because we know, to put our future first,
we must first put our differences aside.
We lay down our arms
so we can reach out our arms
to one another.
We seek harm to none and harmony for all.

When you read these words, you can see the vision of freedom for all that both Presidents Lincoln and Kennedy desired for their country. You can feel the torment and tears felt by people of color. You can see the imprint that it left on humanity especially for those oppressed in the last 400 years and yet this poem that speaks volumes about our history, is banned in schools in the state of Florida. Why? Because they say it teaches children how to be racist. Racism does not come from teaching about our history; it comes from a negative state of mind and the actions that follow this state of mind. Racism is an imaginary boundary that has been taught to humans and is passed down. How can we learn from the past if we cannot even speak or teach the truth?

President Kennedy spoke truth, when he proposed a Civil Rights Bill that prohibits discrimination on the basis of color, race, religion, sex, or national origin. He had a great vision for everyone to be included; included in public schools, included in restaurants, and included other public places. He even wanted for everyone that was an American citizen, regardless of race or color to be able to vote.

As you can see from the days of the first settlers, when they first enslaved the Native Indians, to shipping Africans to America for the sole purpose of slavery, to the hate of Muslims, Asians and immigrants; it has been a hard battle for anyone of color or anyone who is not Christian, like the Jews. Thankfully there were some that had the vision to direct us of this darkness and help us surpass the grips of hatred and racism; but that vision comes with a substantial price.

Sometimes we get so caught up in the imaginary boundaries that we grow up in, that it propels us to do the unthinkable. As was the case for Lee Harvey Oswald who was raised in the Lutheran Church and later became a Marine. It was getting close to Thanksgiving and our country and government were at the beginning stages, trying to adjust to a more diverse type of society. At least that was the vision that the 35th President of the United States had within his soul. That is until November 22, 1963, when racist white man scared of change, named Lee Harvey Oswald assassinated John F. Kennedy from the 6th floor of a building in Dallas, Texas. Oswald used a rifle that he ordered from an American Rifle magazine for just $21.45, with a scope.

Through the scope of the civil rights movements emerged the most prominent leader in American History to ever fight the injustices brought on by racism. Martin Luther King Jr. was a Baptist Minister, a political philosopher, and an activist. But what he is most admired for is speaking the truth and trying to free the masses with his vision.

He was able to capture the hearts and minds of millions with his eloquent wording and expressions of freedom that he held dearly in his heart. Most famous for his "I have a Dream Speech," let us dive into MLK's vision, "I have a dream that my four little children will one day live in a nation where they will not be judged by the color of their skin, but by the content of their character." It's not hard to see why Martin Luther King Jr. won the Nobel Peace Prize award at the young age of thirty-five.

Following in his footsteps and also blessed with the vision is his granddaughter, Yolanda Renee King; who, On the March, in Washington (2023) spoke to the massive crowds. She said, "If I could speak with my grandfather, I would say I'm sorry we still have to be here to rededicate ourselves to finishing your work and ultimately realizing your dream," She went on to say, "Today racism is still with us. Poverty is still with us and now gun violence has come for places of worship, our schools, and our shopping centers."

MLK's son, Martin Luther King III said on that same day, "I'm very concerned about the direction our country is going in… Instead of moving forward, it feels as if we are moving backward." That is because we have a so-called leader that is directing his cult-like followers back to a time when the white man ruled over everyone and everything. Those days are long gone, and I keep writing it and writing it, but we cannot and will not go backwards!

If we could go back in time, I would go back and warn Martin Luther King Jr. to stay away from the Lorraine Motel in Memphis, Tennessee on that April 4th evening, in 1968. I would warn him of a white man who grew up in the Catholic faith by the name of James Earl Ray. I would say brother; a coward with a rifle is going to shoot you today from the building across the street. I would say that he is blinded by the imaginary boundaries of his mind and wants to kill you, because you possess the vision of freedom for all, that they, who are blinded, cannot see.

The great John Lennon grasped these auspicious visions also and conveyed them into a song. He envisioned a world of peace and harmony, a world where all humans were treated equally, a world without borders (walls). A world where there were no

(114)

imaginary boundaries (religions) and a world where we could live as *one*. Imagine, all the people living in peace and living for today. You could say that he was a dreamer, but so was Abraham Lincoln, John F Kennedy, and Martin Luther King Jr., and just like those auspicious dreamers; John Lennon was shot to death on Dec 9, 1980, in New York City, by a white man named Mark David Chapman, a proclaimed born-again Christian.

These four astonishing minds attempted to free humans from the strangleholds and racism of those imaginary boundaries. They sacrificed their lives for our freedoms and each of these men were chosen to deliver the message. Each of those killers murdered the messengers, but the message is still alive!

Sadly, each killer mentioned could not see the vision, because the vision does not dwell in people in search of unauthentic power. It does not dwell in those who judge, control, or attempt to overpower others. It cannot thrive in those who do not love life or are merely passing through. Each of those cowards was blinded by imaginary boundaries. Those four killers mentioned were brought up with the bible and loved their guns, and as long as we have access to guns and people with this discriminatory mindset, we will continue to witness the death of innocence and righteousness.

The same can be said in the story of Jesus, if the political and religious societies of that era had firearms, rest assured that Jesus would have been shot as well. It is time to fully awaken to the auspicious visions that are within us. This is the true awakening, not that fake one that conspiracy theories are trying to lure you into. This one brings freedom for all, and it brings all humans in connection to one another through our common sense. It is this awakening, that is for love, because it is love that conquers all!

Either you are on the side of righteousness and believe that all humans are created equally; or you are on the side of racism and hatred. Either you are for all humans having rights, like woman, gays, trans, and immigrants; or you are on the other side who wants to cast judgement upon them, covert them or give them hell. That is the side that truly divides us and sends us spiraling backwards. In the world in which the far right envisions, there would be no gays, trans, nor people of color; everyone would have firearms and there would be nothing but great walls dividing us, and all religions would convert to a single faith and become white Christian nationalist society.

On the other side of the coin is where the righteous and self-confident reside; where all colors, all religions, all cultures, all creeds are living free, without guns and are treated equally. It's much brighter on this side because we do not hate on anyone. Everyone is included and welcomed. Where one can continuously be reborn and is able to pursue life, liberty and happiness without racism, harassment or abuse.

What side of history do you want to be part of? How do you want to be remembered when they read about us in the future, if we are to survive? Do you want to be remembered as a species that once lived on earth, and then suddenly disappeared because they were too quiet to stand up against the right's extremism and ignorance. Or do you want to take control of your life and your destiny right now and say enough with the Hate!

Every country and every culture has its own beautiful traditions and ceremonies, and we should embrace, appreciate and learn to celebrate them. We need to stop this trend of trying to erase, eradicate and/or acculturate people and replace them with what we feel is best for them. We have lost a lot of collective wisdom and culture in doing this; just like the settlers eroded the ways of the Native Indians. Now, more than ever we must humble ourselves because many of our ways are not working, and that's ok, as long as we can learn from our failures and learn to take note from those who are succeeding. As Aristotle put it, "He who cannot be a good follower, cannot be a good leader."

As we approach the end of this literature, I hope that the auspicious visions that the chosen ones brought forth have ignited your own passion for Freedom. I pray that you will pass this information onto others, because the more that we educate ourselves and color the earth with creativity and unity, the more enhanced our children's lives will be. More than anything, I hope that you can now see life without imaginary boundaries, because if you can, then we have fulfilled the ultimate intentions of the universe and that is to be free! At the signing of the Declaration of Independence, Ben Franklin stood up and said, "We must all hang together, or assuredly we shall all hang separately." Meaning we can choose to become *one* through our common sense, or over our labels we shall perish. We can choose to be one with nature and the universe, or we can choose-

The End!

Book References:
and Special Thanks!

Napoleon Hill   "Think and Grow Rich"
Thomas Moore   "Care for the Soul"
Alice Walker   "Anything can be Saved"
Rowan Robinson   "The great Book of Hemp"
Paul Kurtz   "Forbidden Fruit"
Dr. Wayne W Dyer   "Everyday Wisdom"
Benjamin Franklin   "Poor Richard's Almanac"
Thomas Pane   "Common Sense"
Charles Darwin   "The Origin of Species"
Thomas Jefferson   "Declaration of Independence"

George Washington   Ehud C Sperling
Alan Aloa   William Blake
Abraham Maslow   Nostradamus
Amanda Gorman   Yolanda Rene King
Plato   Martin Luther King Jr III
Abraham Lincoln   Businessinsider.com
Martin Luther King Jr.   Willie Nelson
John Lennon   Dali Lama
Walt Disney   Vicente Fernandez
Henry Ford   Vincent Van Gogh
Albert Einstein   Steve Jobs
Aldous Huxley   Evo Moreles
James Madison   Mother Teresa
Darshil Shah   Lao Tzu
Various Authors   First and Second Testament
Buddha   Oprah Winfrey

Special thanks to Environmental and Energy Study Institute and Everytown for Gun Safety, the CDC, The US Constitution and Declaration of Independence, Netflix, google, YouTube and National Geographic. If I missed anyone, I thank you also for contributing to the knowledge and success of this literature. Thank you so much to all who read this book, I really appreciate all the support, now let's go change the World!

<u>Biography</u>

I started my journey about 10 miles south of the Alamo, in a humble little home with my grandmother and mother. Being part of the community and church was everything for us because my grandmother was the matriarch of our family. Our church is a historic mission similar to the Alamo yet rooted in the Hispanic culture and in the Catholic faith.

Our home was nestled right outside the mission's compound, and we lived in a nice, wooded area. The same woods that the Native Indians once hunted in. I would go into the woods and see the different types of trees, like pecan, oak and mesquite trees, and I would sit and just feel the energy. I knew that I lived directly in a location that was rich in history, I could just feel it. We were often taught that the natives were converted into Christianity to help our ancestors prosper. But what really happened is the natives lost their culture to the Spanish and Spanish to the English.

When I was 6 years old, one of my Uncles came down to visit us and talked about this place that he lived and wanted to take us there, because it was beautiful. So, in 1982 we moved to New Haven, Connecticut. This was different in every way possible from South Texas. I went to a school that was almost all African-American. My best friends were mostly all African-Americans, and I grew up in their culture. I remember the history being taught was different also; for instance, I would do book reports on Harriet Tubman, Rosa Parks, and Malcom X.

We lived at the basin of west rock, which was basically a huge rock that looked like a mountain. The trees here were also different, lots of elm, ash and maple surrounded our home. I remember studying the trees and noticing how they differ in different regions, yet they are all trees. My uncle was a successful business owner, and he owned a convenience store about 5 miles away from Yale University. Because of him I was able to go and see some of the best museums in the world. We would spend many days visiting Manhattan and taking in the history of New York. So, my mind was expanding rapidly.

In school we went on trips to places like Plymouth Rock and I saw firsthand how the first settlers lived. I remember clearly (because they do reenactments of those early days) there were some huge wooden gate doors that led to the woods. So, my friends and I went down the wooded trail to a stream that had real Native Indians playing a drum and singing songs by a little fire. I was amazed because I hadn't seen Native Indians since I lived in San Antonio. The Indians looked right at me and said, "There once was a scorpion and needed to cross the river, so he asked a frog for a ride across, the frog resisted and said you will sting me, the scorpion said, "no I won't, you have my word," so the frog agrees. The scorpion climbs on his back and about midway through, the scorpions begins to sting him, and the frog says, "why would you do that, now we are both going to drown," the scorpion says, "I can't help it, this is who I am." I still remember this story as vividly as the day it was told to me.

Then in 1989 my mother picked up from school on this warm spring day. I remember this day because my computer teacher showed us a movie and said to me, "I need for you to pay close attention to this film." I was taken away by the way he said that, so I paid attention. We saw the film "<u>Stand and Deliver</u>" and I had never really seen Latinos on film before, but it reminded me of what I felt like when I watched "<u>Stand By Me</u>". I knew at that moment that I wanted to be a writer. So, I ran to my uncle's car after school to tell him the good news, only to find my mother crying. She said, "Let's go, Uncle Ruben is in the hospital." It turns out; two New Haven police men dragged him out of his car and beat him nearly to death. It was a hate crime for being Latino and Gay.

This left an imprint on me, and I had to realize that we were still living in a world of ignorance, and even though most people are good, there are some that still hold on to racism and prejudice. My upbringing was a culmination of all of these things, and I am so grateful to my Uncle, for not only showing me the prominence of New England and it's abundant history, but more so, for showing me how to be a good man. I now understand the synchronicity of my childhood, it was to shape my mind and spirit into the one that would deliver the ultimate message – we are all <u>chosen</u>!

That scorpion story is also told in a snake poem, with the same meaning. Trump uses it to describe immigrants on the border and often reads it at his rallies to generate hate against Latinos or immigrants. Trump is the <u>real</u> snake here and I knew when he won in 2016 that our world was going to change and not for the better, and I warned people that this was the worst thing that could have happened for this country. We went from the United States of America to the Divided States of America, but now it is time to wake up and reunite. As Martin Luther King Jr. once said, "Darkness cannot drive out darkness. Only light can do that. Hate cannot drive out hate. Only love can do that."
Choose Love!